Employment Law and Works Councils of the Netherlands

Dutch Business Law

The series Dutch Business Law is a continuous publication in loose-leaf form under the editorial supervision of Steven R. Schuit, a former partner of Allen & Overy and professor of law at Utrecht University and at Nyenrode Business Universiteit.

This current publication is a bound edition of the series previously published in loose-leaf form.

The purpose of Dutch Business Law is to provide a good understanding of the practical implications of the relevant areas of Dutch law under consideration. The authors are seasoned practitioners, experienced in representing international clients in the Dutch legal arena.

This book makes no pretence to be a survey of the entire Dutch business law – either in scope or substance. It contains generalisations and simplications and cannot be regarded as presenting complete and in depth advice in the areas covered.

KLUWER LAW INTERNATIONAL

Employment Law and Works Councils of the Netherlands

By

Ferdinand B.J. Grapperhaus

and

Leonard G. Verburg

Partners at Allen & Overy Amsterdam

Wolters Kluwer
Law & Business

AUSTIN BOSTON CHICAGO NEW YORK THE NETHERLANDS

Published by:
Kluwer Law International
P.O. Box 85889
2508 CN The Hague
The Netherlands
E-mail: sales@kluwerlaw.com
Website: http://www.kluwerlaw.com

Sold and distributed in North, Central and South America by:
Aspen Publishers, Inc.
7201 McKinney Circle
Frederick, MD 21704
USA
E-mail: customer.care@aspenpubl.com

Sold and distributed in all other countries by:
Extenza-Turpin Distribution Services
Stratton Business Park
Pegasus Drive
Biggleswade
Bedfordshire SG18 8TQ
United Kingdom
E-mail: sales@kluwer.com

Printed on acid-free paper

ISBN 978-90-411-2858-4

Preface

The ability to recruit, retain and manage the right people is key to the continued growth and success of a business. As markets become increasingly global and the law affecting employees becomes more complex, the need for management to be cognoscente of its obligations as an employer has never been more critical. Moreover, employing people is a complicated business. Not knowing one's obligations as an employer can be expensive and damaging. Thus, knowledge of employment law and works councils is essential.

This publication contains practical and legal information on the hiring and firing of employees, terms and conditions of employment, workplace issues and the rights of (European) works councils. It offers practical guidance to in-house counsels and lawyers who deal with Dutch labour law and co-determination issues and also can serve to facilitate communication between businessmen and their Dutch counsel.

This book inevitably contains generalisations and should not be regarded as presenting definitive advice, nor is it intended to provide a substitute for expert legal advice. The reader should be aware that the law in this area is constantly changing and that this work reflects the law as stated at the time of writing.

Allen & Overy's Amsterdam Employment Practice Group ('The Group') offers expert advice in all areas of employment and benefits law and is a part of the Allen & Overy's European Employment, Pensions and Incentives Group. The Group is one of the most highly qualified employment and benefits law departments of all major international law firms, with over 130 lawyers located across 13 European centres. By having dedicated teams in key locations, The Group can provide the very best national and international advice with an assurance of consistent quality and effective coordination.

Ferdinand B.J. Grapperhaus
ferdinand.grapperhaus@allenovery.com

Leonard G. Verburg
leonard.verburg@allenovery.com

Amsterdam, September 2008

About the Authors

Ferdinand Grapperhaus has been a partner with Allen & Overy since 2000. He is engaged in employment law both as a litigator as well as a legal counsel. He is most renowned for his work on collective labour disputes, individual employment issues, and boardroom counselling. He also deals frequently with works council issues. Ferdinand is a part-time Employment Law professor at the University of Maastricht. In 1995 he earned his doctors degree on a lengthy study of *Non-competition clauses in Employment Law*. He was appointed by Her Majesty Queen Beatrix as an independent member to the Social Economic Council, the Netherlands primary advisory board on all issues of social-economic policy and legislation. Furthermore, he is a member of the International Association of Insolvency (INSOL) and the Vereniging van Amsterdamse arbeidsrechtadvocaten. He is an editor of the Dutch leading corporate law review *Ondernemingsrecht*. Ferdinand is (co-)author of various books on subjects relating to both Dutch and European Employment Law, such as *The end of the Affair on the ménage à trios of employment, contract and termination*, Deventer: Kluwer 2006; *Equal pay for temporary agency workers, Taking a closer look at the draft directive on working conditions for temporary agency workers*, Deventer: Kluwer 2003; co-author with M. Jansen, *De uitzendovereenkomst*, Monografieën Sociaal Recht nr. 15, Deventer: Kluwer 1999; *Werknemersconcurrentie* (dissertation), Deventer: Kluwer 1995.

Leonard Verburg has been a partner with Allen & Overy LLP since January 2000. He was a partner with Benelux law firm Loeff Claeys Verbeke from 1987. He is a member of the employment law department of the Amsterdam office. He graduated from Leyden University in 1979 and got his Ph.D. in March 2007. He is a professor at Radboud University Nijmegen since August 2007. He has experience of a wide range of employment law-related matters such as individual and collective dismissals, strikes, negotiation with unions and employment contracts (both in an advisory role and regarding litigation). In particular, he has knowledge and experience of works council issues and disputes at board room/executive level. He is editor-in-chief of *ArbeidsRecht*, one of the leading magazines on employment law, and editor of *Arbeidsrechtelijke Annotaties*. Leonard is a member of the standing advisory committee on employment law of the Dutch Bar Association as well as a member of the standing committee of the Arbeidsrecht Congress, the annual gathering of Dutch employment lawyers. Author of *Het territoir van de (Nederlandse) ondernemingsraad in het internationale bedrijfsleven* (Kluwer 2007, dissertation University of Amsterdam) and of *De koers van de bestuurder* (Kluwer 2008). Leonard is co-author and editor of the leading book on reorganisations under Dutch law, *Arbeidsrechtelijke aspecten van reorganisatie* (Kluwer 2008). Over the years he has published numerous articles on employment law and works council issues.

Table of Contents

Part I
Employment Law[1]

1. In cooperation with Liesbeth Franx-Schaap, Alwin Stege, Lucy van den Berg and Catherine Milo.

Chapter 1
Labour Relations

1.1 EMPLOYERS' ASSOCIATIONS

The Federation of Netherlands Industry and Employers (VNO-NCW)[1] is the principal employers' association, made up of some 150 organisations covering nearly every industry sector. One of its members is the General Dutch Employers' Federation (AWVN),[2] which carries out negotiations on collective labour agreements (CLA) (*Collectieve Arbeidsovereenkomst*) on behalf of most employers and their associations. Additionally, a large number of branch organisations have joined the Federation of Small and Medium-Sized Enterprises (*MKB Nederland*).[3] Together, the Federations offer a wide range of interesting services to their members. Membership is not compulsory.

1.2 TRADE UNIONS

More than a quarter of the Dutch labour force, roughly 25 per cent, is unionised.[4] Most of the unions have joined one of the three trade union federations. The largest of these is the Netherlands Trade Union Federation (FNV), which consists of 15 trade unions with a joint membership of 1,181,800.[5] The second largest federation

1. *See* <www.vno-ncw.nl>.
2. *See* <www.awvn.nl>.
3. *See* <www.mkb.nl>.
4. *See* <www.cbs.nl>, the Netherlands Statistics Office (CBS) indicates that in 2007 there were approximately 1.9 million trade union members, whilst the working population in 2007 was approximately 8.6 million.
5. *Source*: Netherlands Statistics Office, membership in 2007, the website of Statistics Netherlands is <www.cbs.nl>. *See* <www.fnv.nl> as well.

is the Federation of Christian Trade Unions (CNV),[6] which is made up of thirteen trade unions with an aggregate membership of 335,200. The third union is the Trade Union Federation for Intermediate and Senior Staff (*Vakcentrale MHP*), which comprises four unions with a joint membership of 167,500.[7] Trade union membership is not compulsory, with the exception of the printing industry where an industry-wide CLA applies under which all its members must have joined one of the unions that are party to the agreement.

1.3 CONSULTATIVE BODIES

Trade unions and employers' associations are the most important national lobbies. In 1945, at the end of World War II, employers and employees established the Labour Foundation (*Stichting van de Arbeid*),[8] in which they try to reach a central settlement on an annual basis which can serve as a guideline for the national negotiations on CLAs.

In addition, there is a consultative and advisory body called the Social and Economic Council[9] (SER) (*Sociaal Economische Raad*) in which employers, employees and the government participate. The Council advises the government and parliament on national and international social and economic issues, and is also involved in upholding the Works Council Act.

1.4 THE FORMATION OF CLAs

A CLA is an agreement primarily dealing with labour conditions. It is entered into by one or more employers or employers' associations and one or more trade unions, usually for a period of one or two years. This differs from a country like the United States, for instance, where a trade union does not have to represent a majority of the workers of an employer to have power to negotiate a CLA.

CLAs can be negotiated on company level, or industry-wide, the latter being more usual. Industry-wide CLAs apply to all the companies in a particular industry sector. Some of the larger Dutch enterprises (Akzo, KPN, Philips) have their own CLAs, which only apply to their own workforce. To become effective a CLA must be registered with the Minister of Social Affairs and Employment, although this requirement is only a formality as the Minister does not assess the contents of the agreement itself.

6. *See* <www.cnv.nl>.
7. *See* <www.vakcentralemhp.nl>.
8. *See* <www.stvda.nl>.
9. *See* <www.ser.nl>.

1.5 THE GENERALLY BINDING CLA

If an employer is not a member of an employers' association which has conducted negotiations on a CLA for any particular branch, it will not as a rule be bound to the outcome of the talks. Nor are its employees. This means that, throughout the period of any individual employment agreement unaffiliated employers and employees do not have to observe the provisions which govern their particular CLA. If, however, the CLA has been declared generally binding, it applies to all employers and employees across a certain business sector, irrespective of membership of a CLA-party. When a collective agreement is declared generally binding it is also binding for the unaffiliated employer.

CLA-provisions may be declared generally binding by the Minister of Social Affairs and Employment,[10] who may only do this at the request of one of the parties involved in the formation of the CLA. An order which declares a collective agreement binding can only apply industry-wide, not for an individual company.

For a long time after the war collective labour bargaining power in the Netherlands was dominated by politics. Government policies prevented free negotiation between employers and trade unions on matters like wage increases. This changed in the seventies. Under international treaties governments are no longer allowed to intervene in collective labour bargaining, even though politicians often try to influence management and labour in order to limit wage increases.

1.6 THE WORKS COUNCIL

As a rule, management determines the day-to-day running of a business. But employees also have a say through their representatives, the most important of which is the works council, whose members are employees elected by their colleagues. Its method of working is set out in the Works Council Act (WOR) (*Wet op de Ondernemingsraden*) (*See infra* Part II-Works Councils).

1.7 STAFF REPRESENTATION

There are two employee participation schemes in place for businesses with fewer than 50 employees. A business with between 10 and 50 staff may establish staff representation of its own accord.[11] If requested by a majority of the staff, the employer has an obligation to agree to this. The obligation to set up staff representation may also come from a CLA or a public labour conditions scheme. The staff representation is elected directly by the employees of the business and

10. Wet op het Algemeen Verbindend en Onverbindend Verklaren van Bepalingen van Collectieve Arbeidsovereenkomsten (Declaration of Universally Binding and Non-binding Status Act), 1937 *as amended.*
11. WOR Art. 35c.

consists of at least three persons. Its powers include: approval of working hours/ schedules [and working conditions, sickness policy and reintegration policy – Article WOR 35c (4) in conjunction with WOR 27 (1) d WOR]; the right to be advised of resolutions that may result in job losses and/or major changes in labour or labour conditions for at least 25 per cent of employees.[12]

Staff representatives also have the right to certain information. If no system of staff representation has been established, management must meet with employees at least twice a year. On at least one of these occasions it must discuss the general affairs of the business. If a decision is proposed that may result in job losses for at least 25 per cent of employees, it must allow the rendering of advice.[13]

A business with fewer than 10 staff may also establish staff representation.[14] The employer only has an obligation to do so when representation has been determined in a CLA or under a public labour conditions scheme. If staff representation is established, it has the same powers as the staff representation for a business with between 10 and 50 staff.[15]

1.8 STRIKES

As a rule, trade unions do not call strikes unreasonably, and once called, strikes are often short. Only rarely do workers strike for more than three consecutive days. In 2006, some 16,000 working days were lost due to strikes, involving some 11,000 workers. In 2007, these figures were 26,000 working days, with 21,000 workers involved.[16]

No specific Dutch law gives employees the right to strike when, *e.g.* their trade union fails to conclude a collective agreement with their employer. However, the European Social Charter (ESC) of 1961 recognises the right of employees and employers to undertake collective action, including strikes and lock-outs.

In 1986, the Supreme Court ruled that Article 6 ESC is directly applicable in the Netherlands.[17] This means that the Dutch government does not have to implement this provision under Dutch Civil Code. Employers and employees undertaking collective action are shielded by this provision. In short, a strike is considered legitimate action when used as the ultimate weapon when dealing with wages and/ or employment conditions and it is to be used only after a breakdown in serious negotiations. Political strikes aimed at the government – *e.g.* because of a Bill pending in Parliament which will have an impact on workers' rights – can also be

12. WOR Art. 35b(5).
13. WOR Art. 35b.
14. WOR Art. 35d.
15. WOR Art. 35d(2).
16. The figures are derived from Centraal bureau voor de Statistiek (the Netherlands Statistics Office), *see* <www.cbs.nl >.
17. Judgment of 30 May 1986, Hoge Raad [HR] (Supreme Court), 1986 Nederlandse Jurisprudentie [NJ] (Dutch Court Reporter) No. 688.

lawful, and there is nothing the employer can do about such strikes.[18] Political strikes bearing no relation to workers' rights are usually unlawful.

In December 2000 the European Council, the European Commission and the European Parliament signed the Charter of Fundamental Rights of the European Union.[19] The right to undertake collective action is included in this Charter, so it is considered a fundamental right in the European Union. However, employers and employees cannot claim any direct rights from this Charter, because its status is not entirely clear. Still, it is expected that the Court of Justice of the European Communities will use the Charter for guidance whenever suitable.

Although the ESC recognises the right to undertake collective action, there are still situations in which a strike can be unlawful. For example, a strike can be a breach of contract if there is a CLA which is applicable. It is not unusual for parties to a CLA to agree not to undertake collective action for the duration of the agreement.

In addition to the possibility of breach of contract, a strike can also be unlawful if the conflict is not between the employer and its employees, but between a business partner of the employer and its employees. These 'sympathy' or 'solidarity' strikes have generally been held to be unlawful. Strikes and related collective actions may also be unlawful if they cause damage disproportionate to the interests of the non-striking workers or third parties. However, the Supreme Court considers that the aim of the strike is to hurt the employer, so the employer will have to accept the usual damages.

Picketing is uncommon in the Netherlands. Case law shows that blockades, the closing-off of an entrance gate, obstruction of employees and other forms of intimidation are usually considered unlawful. Often striking employees register with their trade union to apply for compensation. An employer does not have any obligation to pay employees who are on strike. In addition, striking employees are not entitled to unemployment benefit. This explains why most strikes end within a few days. The employer is allowed to lock out employees who are not striking if they cannot perform their duties because of the strike. If the non-striking employees have an interest in the strike, *e.g.* because the strike is about wage increases for all employees, they are not entitled to their usual pay, even though they are not on strike themselves.

It is uncommon for employers to hire replacement workers. Hiring of temporary workers to break strikes is also not an option, and the law forbids temporary staffing agencies to send workers as replacement staff where collective action is taking place.[20]

---

18. Judgment of 11 Nov. 1994, HR, 1995 NJ No. 152.
19. Charter of Fundamental Rights of the European Union, Official Journal of the European Communities [O.J. EUR. COMM.] (No. 364) 1 (2000).
20. Wet allocatie arbeidskrachten door intermediairs (Placement of Personnel by Intermediaries Act), 1998, Art. 10.

Chapter 2
Staffing

2.1 ADVERTISEMENTS AND/OR RECRUITMENT AGENCIES

Employees are usually recruited through advertisements, through an intermediary like the public Work and Income Agency (*Centrum voor Werk en Inkomen*), or private recruitment agencies. The services of the Work and Income Agency are free of charge for both employer and employee. These services include information on wages and labour conditions in specific industries. The Work and Income Agency has about 150 regional offices. Employees who have lost their jobs must register at the Work and Income Agency as a prerequisite to obtaining unemployment benefits.

2.2 TEMPORARY STAFFING

The high degree of job protection (*see infra* Chapter 6) makes it difficult for employers to swiftly put into effect any changes which effect the workforce in response to, say, changes in the economic situation. Therefore, employers often make use of temporary workers in order to achieve a certain degree of flexibility. The temporary staffing agreement has been defined by law[1] as an employment agreement under which an employer, within the framework of its profession or enterprise, puts an employee at the disposal of a third party in order to perform work under the supervision and guidance of such third party, and on the basis of a mandate given by such third party to the employer. In effect the law states that the relationship between an employment agency and a temporary employee qualifies

1. Burgerlijk Wetboek [BW] (Civil Code), Art. 7:690.

as an employment agreement. No employment agreement comes into existence between the third-party principal and the temporary employee. However, should such a relationship come into existence it entails certain rights and obligations for the principal and the temporary employee, such as liability for damages caused by the temporary employee during the performance of his work. It sometimes happens that the principal decides to employ the temporary employee for a specific period of time. In the event that the employee continues to perform the same or similar work after that period of time has elapsed, the period during which the employee previously worked as a temporary employee for this particular principal are included when calculating the chain of contracts and the duration of contracts for a fixed period (*see infra* Section 6.3). The legal provisions specifically relating to the temporary employment agreement do not apply to contracting out within the same group of companies, or to examples of contracting out when the temporary employment agency retains guidance and supervision over the working activities of the employee for the employer.

2.3 EMPLOYMENT OF THE DISABLED

The Equal Treatment (Handicapped and Chronically Ill People) Act (Wet gelijke behandeling op grond van handicap of chronische ziekte, 2003) imposes an obligation on employers, organisations of employers, and unions, to provide, in so far as it is within their power, equal opportunities for disabled employees and non-disabled employees, and to improve working conditions. Article 4 Working Conditions Act (Arbowet) requires employers to take care of an adequate working place, working methods and instruments for the handicapped or chronically ill employee. The Act aims to help workers recover and regain their ability to work. On the basis of the Work and Income (Ability to Work) Act (Wet Werk en Inkomen naar Arbeidsvermogen (WIA)) employers can be subsidised for amendments they have to make for these employees.

2.4 EQUAL TREATMENT

On the basis of the Equal Opportunities Act (*Wet Gelijke Behandeling Mannen en Vrouwen*, 1980) and the Dutch Civil Code,[2] discrimination between men and women at any stage of employment is prohibited. This includes advertisement of vacancies, engagement of employees, promotion (or any other opportunity), wages, fringe benefits, pension rights and decision-making relating to dismissal procedures. Discrimination can take place either directly or indirectly. Direct discrimination on the basis of gender means that an employer is influenced by the fact of dealing with a male or female employee. Indirect discrimination means

2. BW Arts 7:646 and 7:648.

discrimination on criteria other than the gender of an employee, *e.g*. full-time or part-time work, which may result in discrimination on the basis of gender. Indirect discrimination can be allowed where the difference in treatment of men and women is justifiable, irrespective of the gender of the employee.

If an employer acts contrary to the principle of non-discrimination an employee may claim damages or salary arrears. The employee may also appeal to the Equal Treatment Committee (Commissie Gelijke Behandeling). However, this committee has no sanctions available to it other than publishing an opinion of the case. If an employer gives notice of termination in violation of the principle of non-discrimination, the employee may invoke its nullity under the Act within two months of receipt of notice.

The Equal Treatment Act (*Algemene Wet Gelijke Behandeling*, 1994) prohibits discrimination on the basis of religion, race, gender, nationality, marital status, political conviction, philosophy of life and sexual orientation at any stage of employment. Sanctions for non-compliance with this Act, are similar to those applicable in case of violation of the Equal Opportunities Act and the equal treatment provisions under the Dutch Civil Code. In the event of a difference in interpretation between the Equal Opportunities Act and the equal treatment provisions of the Dutch Civil Code, versus the Equal Treatment Act, the provisions of the former will apply.

The Age Discrimination Act (Wet gelijke behandeling op grond van leeftijd bij de arbeid, 2004) prohibits discrimination on the basis of age at certain stages of employment. Direct as well as indirect discrimination is allowed where the difference in treatment on the basis of age is justifiable, irrespective of the age of the employee.

Most equal treatment acts also include a ban on intimidation.

2.5 TRANSFER OF A BUSINESS UNDERTAKING

The Transfer of Undertakings Act (*Wet overgang van onderneming*) is designed to implement Dutch obligations under the EC's Acquired Rights Directive. The Act[3] protects employees' rights when all or part of the enterprise, or the part in which they work, is transferred. Broadly speaking, the employees will in the eyes of the law automatically move with the enterprise, retaining the same terms and conditions of employment with the new employer as they had prior to the transfer. As from 1 July 2002 this also applies with respect to pension rights. Written, as well as verbal agreements will be transferred. In the event that court proceedings are in progress at the time of transfer, the transfer will have consequences on the proceedings, and the proceedings will transfer along with the employee being transferred. Employment conditions that are set out in a CLA but not in an individual employment agreement, will also be transferred to the transferee. This implies that

3. Implemented in BW Arts 7:662-666.

the provisions in the CLA will remain in force for the transferred employee until such time as the CLA expires. The Transfer of Undertakings Act does not apply if the transferring company has been declared bankrupt.

2.6 FOREIGN EMPLOYEES: VISA AND (WORK) PERMITS

Essentially the same rules apply to foreigners employed in the Netherlands as to Dutch citizens. There are, however, a few exceptions. In many cases foreign nationals must obtain permits, and may be eligible for special tax treatment. Moreover, in certain cases their employment agreements may be governed by foreign law (*see infra* Section 3.4). Citizens of several countries require a visa to enter the Netherlands for less than three months. This does not apply to citizens of the European Union (EU) and the European Economic Area (EEA),[4] who can enter the Netherlands with only a valid passport.[5]

Based on the EU principles of free movement, citizens of the EU and the EEA are allowed to stay and work in the Netherlands. Citizens from EU/EEA Member States neither need a residence permit or a work permit to be allowed to work in the Netherlands. There is an exception for the citizens from the new Member States Romania and Bulgaria: these citizens have to apply for a work permit, but not for a residence permit.[6] For the purpose of showing proof of legal residence, the Immigration and Naturalisation Service (Immigratie- en Naturalisatiedienst), the IND, can affix a sticker to a passport on request. After a stay of three months citizens of EU/EEA Member States are required to register with the IND.

There are two procedures for employers who wish to employ people from outside the EU and EEA: admission as a labour migrant and admission as a highly skilled migrant. In both cases it concerns hiring someone as an employee.

Admission as a labour migrant pertains to employees who will at least earn the social assistance standard. The employer will have to prove that he has tried to recruit in the EEA, but was not able to find employees there. The employer can then apply for a work permit (*tewerkstellingsvergunning, twv*) with the Centre for Work and Income (CWI) as well as for advice from the IND for a provisional residence permit (*machtiging tot voorlopig verblijf, mvv*). Foreigners from Australia, Canada, the USA and South Korea do not require a provisional residence permit. After positive advice from the IND, foreigners from other countries can submit an application for a provisional residence permit to the Dutch embassy or consulate. When

4. Citizens of the EU and the EEA are defined as citizens of Austria, Belgium, Bulgaria, Czech Republic, Cyprus, Denmark, Estonia, Finland, France, Germany, Greece, Hungary, Iceland, Ireland, Italy, Latvia, Liechtenstein, Lithuania, Luxembourg, Malta, Norway, Poland, Portugal, Romania, Slovenia, Slovakia, Spain, Sweden, the United kingdom and the Netherlands.
5. Source: *Immigratiedienst* (Immigration Service), brochure Visa for a temporary stay, *see* <www.immigratiedienst.nl>.
6. Source: <www.werk.nl>, the site of CWI, and <www.ind.nl>.

the employee is in the Netherlands, he can apply for a more permanent residence permit at the IND office in his region.[7]

The other option is admission as highly skilled migrants. This pertains to employees who will earn an annual income of at least EUR 46,541 (for those older than 30 years of age) or at least EUR 34,130 (for those younger than 30, figures over 2007). The employer has to sign a statement in which he assumes financial responsibility for the foreigner. The advantages of this procedure are that the employer does not have to apply for a work permit and that the IND will decide on the request for advice on the provisional residence permit and residence permit at very short notice. Again, foreigners from Australia, Canada, the USA and South Korea[8] do not require a provisional residence permit.

7. Source: <www.ind.nl>, > Residence Wizard > brochures/forms.
8. Source: <www.ind.nl>, > Residence Wizard > brochures/forms.

Chapter 3
Employment Agreement: General

3.1 DEFINITION

An employment agreement is an agreement under which one party (the employee) undertakes to perform work in the employment of another party (the employer) during a certain period of time and in consideration of a certain payment. Usually, the employer is a legal person or a partnership, but may also be a natural person. The employee is always considered a natural person. The most important criteria applied to establish whether an agreement qualifies as an employment agreement is whether the employer has the right to give instructions with respect to the kind of activities to be performed.

3.2 FORM

An employment agreement can be either oral or written. However, there are some binding provisions which may apply pursuant to a CLA. Certain provisions can only be validly agreed upon in writing (*see infra* Sections 4.1, 4.2 and 3.6). Moreover, the law[1] states that the employer is under an obligation to provide certain information in writing to the employee with respect to the employment agreement. This relates to place of work, job title, date the employment agreement enters into force, remuneration, working hours, terms and conditions relating to holidays and the applicability of any CLA.

1. BW Art. 7:655.

3.3 LEGAL PRESUMPTION OF EMPLOYMENT AGREEMENT

A person who performs paid work for the benefit of another person (natural person, legal person or partnership), for three consecutive months, either weekly or for not less than 20 hours per month, is presumed to perform such work pursuant to a contract of employment.[2] Where a contract of employment has lasted for at least three months, the contracted work in any given month is presumed to amount to the average working period per month over the three preceding months.[3]

3.4 GOVERNING LAW

In principle, parties to an employment agreement are free to choose the governing law[4] of the agreement. Whether this right also includes the right to choose the law of a country with which the employment agreement does not have any actual connection is unclear. The EC convention on the Law Applicable to Contractual Obligations limits the effects of any choice of law in international employment agreements, to the extent that the employee will not lose protection on the basis of mandatory provisions of the law of any country which would apply if no choice of law would have been made.[5] Mandatory rules are legal provisions which can not be contracted out. For example, many provisions of Netherlands law regarding the termination of an employment agreement are considered to be mandatory. In the event that the parties to an employment agreement have not made any choice of law, the law of the country in which the employee usually performs his working activities will apply, at least in principle. If it is not possible to establish which country this is, the law of the country of the employer's principal place of business will be applicable. However, if it appears that, based on all relevant circumstances, the employment agreement has a closer connection with another country, the law of that other country will apply.[6]

3.5 MANDATORY PROVISIONS

The parties to an employment agreement are limited to negotiating their own terms. Both the law and any applicable CLAs (*see infra* Section 1.5) contain mandatory

2. BW Art. 7:610a.
3. BW Art. 7:610b.
4. Judgment of 8 June 1973, HR, 1973 NJ No. 400; EC convention on the Law Applicable to Contractual Obligations, Rome, 19 June 1980 and as of 17 December 2009 the successor of the Convention of Rome 1980: Regulation Rome I, Regulation 593/2008, L 177/6, OJ 4 July 2008.
5. EC Convention on the Law Applicable to Contractual Obligations, Rome 19 June 1980, Art. 6(1).
6. EC Convention on the Law Applicable to Contractual Obligations, Rome 19 June 1980, Art. 6(2); Judgment of 8 June 1973, HR, 1973 NJ No. 400.

rules concerning wages and conditions of employment. If an employment agreement is governed by a CLA, employer and employee are free – within the boundaries of mandatory rules of law – to negotiate improvements in the terms of the CLA, unless the CLA contains a prohibition to this effect.

3.6 CHANGE OF EMPLOYMENT AGREEMENT

The consent of both employer and employee is required to change an employment agreement. However, it is possible to provide in writing that the employer has the right to change the employment agreement without the consent of the employee. The law[7] states that the employer can only make use of this provision if changing the employment agreement is of such importance that, on the basis of reasonableness and fairness, the employer's interest prevails over that of the employee, even though the employee's interests may be harmed by changing the agreement. If such unilateral right to change the employment agreement has not been stipulated by the employer, the employee can under certain circumstances be forced by court order to accept a change of the agreement. The Dutch Supreme Court has held that an employee should generally react positively to reasonable proposals by the employer based on a change of circumstances, and that the employee may only reject such proposals if acceptance of them cannot reasonably be expected of him.[8]

---

7. BW Art. 7:613.
8. Judgment of 26 June 1998, HR, 1998 Jurisprudentie Arbeidsrecht [JAR] (Court Reporter Employment Law) 199.

Chapter 4
Employment Agreement: Terms and Conditions

4.1 DURATION: TRIAL PERIOD

An employment agreement may be concluded for a fixed (*see infra* Section 6.3) or indefinite period (*see infra* Section 6.4) of time. At the start of their relationship the parties to an employment agreement may agree to a trial period. This agreement must be in writing in order to be valid. The duration of the trial period depends on the duration of the employment agreement. If an employment agreement is for two years or more, the trial period is two months. If the employment agreement is for less than two years, the trial period is one month. During this trial period, either party may terminate the employment agreement without prior notice and without a CWI permit (*see infra* Section 6.7).

4.2 RESTRICTIVE COVENANTS

a Confidentiality

An employee may be under an obligation not to disclose confidential information concerning the employer's business either on the basis of a statutory provision or on the basis of a written agreement between employer and employee. The employer may require the employee to sign a confidentiality clause. Confidentiality clauses may be backed-up by a penalty clause. A breach of confidentiality concerning the enterprise is punishable by criminal sanctions.[1]

1. Wetboek van Strafrecht (Dutch Criminal Code) Arts 272 and 273.

b Non-competition

An employee may be prohibited from performing or engaging in activities similar to those of the employer by a written agreement between the employer and the employee.[2] Non-competition agreements may also specifically refer to certain customers or suppliers and may be restricted to certain precisely described products or activities. Moreover, a non-competition agreement may be restricted to a specific geographical area. A competition clause must be agreed upon in writing in order to be valid. An employer loses his rights to non-competition under the clause if he is liable to pay damages because of the termination of the employment. It is generally accepted that the maximum, reasonable time for a non-competition agreement to remain in force is one year after termination of an employment agreement. A non-competition clause only pertains to the employment agreement in force at the date of conclusion of the clause. At the request of the employee the court may limit the scope of the non-competition agreement or ignore it altogether. The court may rule that the employer must pay financial compensation for the duration of the restriction of the employee's activities, if the non-competition clause seriously restricts the employee from accepting other employment.

c Protection of Intellectual Property Rights

i Patents

The rights with respect to inventions created by the employee during employment are governed by the Patent Act 1995.[3] Generally speaking, an employee is entitled to patent rights with respect to his own inventions, unless it follows from the nature of the employment that the employee has been hired to make use of his particular knowledge to create inventions for the benefit of the employer. If this is the case, the employer is entitled to the patent. The employer and employee may vary the above by an agreement in writing. In the event that an inventor who is not entitled to the patent does not receive sufficient compensation – whether in the form of salary or otherwise – the party who is entitled to the patent is under an obligation to pay financial compensation to the inventor. The amount of this compensation should be reasonable and fair in view of the financial importance of the invention and the circumstances under which the invention has been created.

ii Copyrights

The employer is regarded as being the owner of any copyright with respect to works of literature, science or art created by the employee in the course of his

2. BW Art. 7:653.
3. Rijksoctrooiwet [ROW] (Patent Act) 1995 Art. 12.

employment, unless the parties agree otherwise.[4] *In the course of employment* means: in the course of the employee's performance of his job, which must include the production of these works.

These provisions are not mandatory and it is possible to make other arrangements.

d Penalty

Employment agreements may contain penalty clauses. Penalty clauses in employment agreements will only be valid if they have been agreed in writing and if it has been clearly provided which provisions should have been violated for the penalty to be forfeited. Additionally, penalty clauses should provide for the benefit of whomever the penalty will effect – unless expressly excluded – as well as the amount of the penalty.[5] The possibility of enforcing a penalty clause does not preclude the right to claim full compensation of damages on the basis of the law instead.[6]

4.3 MINIMUM WAGES AND MINIMUM HOLIDAY ALLOWANCE

All workers are entitled to a minimum wage and a minimum holiday allowance.[7] The minimum wage as at 1 July 2008 is EUR 1,356.60 gross per month for employees of 23 years of age and older.[8] Employees younger than 23 are entitled to a percentage of this minimum wage. The minimum wage is adjusted on 1 January and 1 July of each calendar year. Most workers earn considerably more than the minimum wage. The average gross monthly pay in August 2008, inclusive of fringe benefits, for employees for whom a collective bargaining agreement was applicable, was EUR 2,460.[9]

Employees are entitled to an annual holiday allowance. The statutory minimum holiday allowance is 8 per cent of the annual gross salary. In so far as the salary of the employee may be in excess of three times the minimum wage, the employee is not entitled by law to holiday allowance on the excess amount. However, the employer and the employee may agree otherwise. Where the salary of the employee exceeds three times the minimum wage, employer and employee may agree in writing that no holiday allowance is payable by the

---

4. Art. 7 Auteurswet (Copyright Act), Art. 7, 1912, *as amended.*
5. BW Art. 7:650.
6. BW Art. 7:651.
7. Wet minimumloon en minimumvakantiebijslag (Minimum Wage and Minimum Holiday Allowance Act), 1968, *as amended.*
8. Source: <www.minszw.nl>.
9. Source: <http://statline.cbs.nl>.

employer at all. Whatever holiday allowance is agreed, that allowance is usually paid in the month of June of each calendar year, but the employer and the employee are at liberty to agree otherwise.

4.4 WORKING HOURS

According to the basic rule of the Working Hours Act[10] (WHA), an employee is only allowed to work a maximum of 12 hours per shift, making a maximum of 60 hours per week, and in a period of 16 weeks 48 hours maximum per week. It is possible to deviate from this basic rule by a CLA or an agreement which has the approval of the works council. For example, this agreement may determine that an employee is allowed to work 10 hours per day, in a period of four weeks, or 50 hours per week; and in a period of 13 weeks, 45 hours per week. Working hours agreed to in employment agreements usually vary between 36 and 40 hours per week for a full-time job.

The WHA also contains rules with respect to overtime, nightshifts and rest periods. In principle, employees do not work on Sundays, unless there is a particular need dictated by the nature of the business. The employee is entitled to at least 13 non-working Sundays annually.

The WHA prohibits child labour. A child is defined as any person under 16 years of age. Children older than 14 years of age are allowed to work only in addition to or in connection with their education.

4.5 HOLIDAYS

The statutory minimum holiday entitlement is based on the number of full working days per week. The normal entitlement is four times the number of working hours per week.[11] A longer period can be fixed by the CLA, the individual employment agreement, or after consultation with the employer. The employer must allow the employee to take a holiday of at least two full consecutive weeks, or two complete but separate weeks, each year. The remaining holidays must be taken in days or hours. The employer must determine the dates of the holiday days in agreement with the employee's wishes, unless prevented by serious reasons. The employee should make his requested holiday dates known to the employer in writing. If the employer does not give good reason for a refusal within 14 days those holidays will be given to the employee as per his or her request.[12] The employer may change the stipulated holiday period, after consultation with the employee, if there is a serious reason, or an emergency, but must pay any resulting costs. Holidays in excess of

---

10. Arbeidstijdenwet, 2007, *as amended.*
11. BW Art. 7:634.
12. BW Art. 7:638.

the statutory minimum may be bought off if this has been agreed upon by the employer and the employee. The employment agreement may contain a provision that sick days can be considered holidays on the condition that the employee retains the statutory minimum holiday entitlement. Unused holiday days lapse after five years.[13]

4.6 PAYMENT OF SALARY DURING SICKNESS

Employees are entitled to 70 per cent of their current salary and no more than 70 per cent of the maximum daily wage as referred to in the Social Insurance Funding Act (*Wet financiering sociale verzekeringen, Wfsv*)[14] during the first 104 weeks of sickness. It is not unusual in the Netherlands for the employer to make up the deficit by paying up to 100 per cent of the salary [over the first year and 70 per cent over the second year]. If the sickness has been caused by an intentional act, omission or the deliberate recklessness of the employee, or if the employee hinders his recovery or refuses to fill another suitable job which he is able to perform, the employee is not in principle entitled to payment or may even be dismissed.

After the second year of sickness, the employee may be entitled to a disability benefit.[15] Employer and employee are, however, required by law to fulfil a number of obligations aimed at reintegrating the employee. Non-performance of these obligations by the employee may result in discontinuation of salary payments or dismissal. Non-performance by the employer can lead to an increase of the length of time salary is paid.

4.7 HEALTH AND SAFETY

The Working Conditions Act (WCA)[16] imposes a general duty on the employer to ensure and improve the safety, health and well-being of his own employees, as well as any employees sub-contracted from other companies or job agencies. One of the obligations is to compile a risk inventory and make an evaluation of the safety, health and risks to well-being at work. Furthermore, the use of instruments, machinery, apparatus and other equipment, as well as the use of materials that may be hazardous to employees' health and safety, must be avoided. More specific rules have been laid down in separate ministerial directives. The Working Conditions Service (*Arbodienst*) can provide information on the specific rules applicable.

---

13. BW Art. 7:642.
14. EUR 159 on 1 Jan. 2002.
15. On the basis of the Disability Insurance Act (WIA). The amount of the benefit is 70 per cent of the latest salary and no more than 70 per cent of the maximum daily wage, which is EUR 179.90 on 1 July 2008.
16. Arbeidsomstandighedenwet 1998.

The WCA requires all employers to join a certified service institute of experts on working conditions (*Arbodienst*). This can be either an internal or an external service. The *Arbodienst* assists the employer in the event of absenteeism due to illness and it provides support for sick and disabled employees. The employer and the *Arbodienst* are obliged to have an active policy on absenteeism. The Health and Safety Inspectorate (*Arbeidsinspectie*) enforces the WCA and its ministerial directives and supervises the *Arbodienst.*

Under the Dutch Civil Code,[17] an employer is obliged to ensure safety in the workplace for his own employees and employees on loan from another company or a job agency. The employer is responsible for accidents which occur in an unsafe workplace unless he can prove that he had fulfilled all safety obligations, or that the accident at work was caused by the deliberate recklessness of the employee. If an employee has an accident and it is shown that the employer did not provide a safe and healthy environment, or failed to secure the safety, health and well-being of the employees, it will be very difficult – or even impossible – for the employer to avoid liability.

4.8 SPECIAL LEAVE

a Maternity and Adoption Leave[18]

Female workers have the right to maternity leave of 16 weeks. Adoption gives a right to leave of four consecutive weeks in the 18-week period commencing two weeks before the day the child is adopted. During maternity or adoption leave the employee has a right to maternity or adoption benefit of 100 per cent of current salary but no more than 100 per cent of the maximum daily wage (per 1 July 2008 EUR 179.90).

b Parental Leave

The Work and Care Act[19] provides that all employees, male and female, regardless of the number of their working hours per week, may take unpaid part-time leave of up to six months when they have to care for a child under eight years of age. A multiple birth, or adoption of more than one child at the same time, gives the right to full parental leave for each child. The employee's weekly working hours may be reduced to a minimum of 50 per cent of his/her weekly working hours for a maximum of six months. No wages are paid for the hours during which the employee is on leave, and after the period of leave the employee should return to the original number of working hours. To be entitled to parental leave the employee

17. BW Art. 7:658.
18. Wet Arbeid en Zorg [WAZO] (Work and Care Act), 2001, Art. 2.1-3.
19. WAZO Arts 6.1-9.

must have been employed by the same employer for more than one year. Except when the employer has substantial grounds on which to refuse, the employee is entitled to take his parental leave over a longer period than six months, or for more than 50 per cent of his/her working hours per week's leave. However, the total hours of leave should not exceed 13 times the employee's normal working hours per week. Parental leave may be divided into three periods of at least one month each. A request to take parental leave must be made in writing at least two months in advance.

c Time-Off for Domestic Emergencies

The Work and Care Act[20] provides for the right of all employees to take a reasonable amount of time off to deal with a domestic incident or any incident which affects a dependant or a member of the employee's immediate family. Employees are entitled to their regular wages during this time off which should usually be for not more than one day.

d Short-Term Care Leave

An employee is entitled to short-term care leave for twice the number of working hours per week (*e.g.* 10 days for a 40-hour work week) per 12-month period.[21] To qualify for this leave, the employee must prove that he/she is caring for a child who is living at home, a foster child, or a partner who cannot be cared for by anyone other than the employee. The employer can object to the employee taking short-term care leave on grounds of business interests which outweigh the interests of the employee. During the period of leave the employee is entitled to 75 per cent of his/her pay as long as this does not exceed the maximum hourly wage set out by national insurance laws. However, it must be at least equal to the minimum wage.

4.9 ADJUSTMENT OF WORKING HOURS

The Adjustment of WHA[22] allows an employee to request adjustment of his or her working hours. The request may be either to increase or reduce the number of working hours. The employee can only make such a request if he/she has been employed by the same employer for at least one year when the requested change is to begin. A request can only be made once every two years. The employer and the employee must consult about the request. The employer must then approve the request for the adjustment unless particularly important business interests prevail.

---

20. WAZO Art. 4.1.
21. WAZO Arts 5.1-10.
22. Wet aanpassing Arbeidsduur (Adjustment of Working Hours Act), 2000.

The Act states that the rules regarding the increase of working hours may be varied by CLA, a written agreement with the works council, or a ministerial directive.

4.10 OLD-AGE PENSIONS AND EARLY RETIREMENT

More than 80 per cent of employees in the Netherlands have the benefit of a pension scheme, provided by employers or their respective industry sectors. Most pension schemes provide for a retirement pension and a widow's and orphan's pension. These pension schemes are supplemental to the statutory pension arrangements contained in the General Old-Age Pensions Act (*Algemene Ouderdomswet*). In addition to these pension arrangements, many industry sectors and businesses have early retirement schemes (VUT), which enable employees to retire before the normal pensionable retirement age. Additionally, there are pre-pension schemes which apply temporarily in the event that a VUT is abolished. In the Netherlands there is no wide-spread obligation to have a pension arrangement in place. This means that employers are generally not under an obligation to have a pension scheme, which becomes a matter of contractual negotiation between employer and employee. In most cases, pension schemes are based on CLAs between employers and trade unions. The CLA usually contains provisions with respect to pensions and the rights and obligations of employer and employee are generally contained in a pension regulation. Some industry sectors have an industry pension fund. Participation in an industry pension fund can be prescribed on a mandatory basis for all employers and employees by the Minister of Social Affairs and Employment Matters, if requested by a sufficiently representative sample of enterprises in the respective industry sector.

In the event that an employer already has a pension scheme for his employees, the provisions of the Pensions Act (*Pensioen-en Spaarfondsenwet*) will apply. The most important obligation under this Act is the requirement to engage a third party for the administration and execution of the scheme. The Pensions Act also obliges the operator of the pension scheme to provide information regarding the employee's pension.

VUTs do not qualify as pension schemes. Consequently, the pension legislation does not apply to VUTs. A VUT generally enables an employee to retire between the ages of 60 and 64. The Dutch Government has argued expressly that expensive early retirement schemes should be replaced by less expensive pre-pension schemes which qualify as pension schemes. According to Dutch tax legislation a pre-pension scheme may only be in operation for a short period of time. Pre-pension payments may amount to no more than 85 per cent of current salary.

Chapter 5
Employment Agreement of Managing Directors

5.1 APPOINTMENT

The two most frequently used forms of legal entity under Netherlands law are the limited liability company (N.V. or *Naamloze Vennootschap*) and the private limited liability company (B.V. or *Besloten Vennootschap*). The members of the management board of an N.V. or B.V. are appointed by the general shareholders' meeting or in the case of a 'large' company by the Supervisory Board. A relationship between a member of the management and the company is subject to both company and employment law. In most cases, members of the management board will not only have been appointed as managing directors under the articles of association, but will also have an employment agreement with the company. The terms and the conditions of their employment are established at the shareholders meeting unless otherwise provided by the articles of association.[1]

5.2 SUSPENSION

Members of the management board can be suspended at any time by the corporate body authorised by the articles of association (general meeting of shareholders or supervisory board).[2] Prior to being suspended, a managing director should be given the opportunity to present his case and to give advice in the shareholders' meeting.

1. BW Art. 2:135/245.
2. BW Art. 2:134/244.

5.3 REMOVAL: TERMINATION OF EMPLOYMENT AGREEMENT

Looked at from the perspective of employment law the position of a managing director of an N.V. or B.V. differs from the position of an ordinary employee. The most important difference is that the employment agreement of a managing director of an N.V. or B.V. can be terminated without the approval of the CWI,[3] a governmental body (*see infra* Section 6.4) The employment agreement of a managing director can be terminated by resolution of the corporate body which appointed him.[4] If the company has a works council, the advice of the works council should be requested prior to terminating the employment agreement.[5] In an increasing number of cases, the so-called Cantonal Court Formula (*see infra* Section 6.9) is applied to establish the amount of compensation a managing director will receive at termination of contract. Best practice principle II.2.7 of the Dutch Corporate Governance Code determines that the maximum severance amount for a managing director should be one year's salary. This code of conduct applies to listed companies only. A listed company can deviate from the principles of the Corporate Governance Code, but will have to state that in its annual report ('the apply or explain principle').[6] A managing director also has the right to claim damages if termination of the employment agreement appears to be obviously unreasonable (*see infra* Section 6.9). Unlike an ordinary employee, a managing director cannot obtain a court order stating that his employment agreement will be restored. Many employment agreements for managing directors include a provision with respect to the financial compensation to be paid to a managing director at termination. However, these types of provisions can be left beyond application by a court. Case law of the Dutch Supreme Court has also introduced a prohibition on giving notice of termination of the employment agreement of a managing director during illness.[7] Although the shareholders have the right to dismiss the managing director from his statutory position during a period of illness, his contract of employment will generally continue to be in full force and effect. The employment agreement of a managing director of an N.V. or B.V. may also be terminated by the District Court if there is serious cause (*see infra* Section 6.8). The managing director of an N.V. or B.V., should be given the opportunity to present his case and to give advice in the shareholders' meeting prior to dismissal.

3. *Centrale Organisatie Werk en Inkomen (Central Organization for Work and Income).*
4. BW Art. 2:134/244.
5. WOR Art. 30(1).
6. Corporate Governance Committee, The Dutch corporate governance code, Principles of good corporate governance and best practice provisions, 9 December 2003. *See also* <www.commissiecorporategovernance.nl>.
7. Judgment of 13 Nov. 1992, HR, 1993 NJ No. 265.

Chapter 6

Suspension and Termination of Employment

6.1 SUSPENSION

There are no specific statutory provisions with respect to suspension (for 'regular' employees, that is, for managing directors of an N.V./B.V. Articles 2:134/2:244 of the Dutch Civil Code apply). Employees may be suspended from their jobs if an employer has urgent, serious reasons that override the interests of the employee in continuing to perform his job.[1] The term of suspension must be as short as possible. The reason(s) for suspension must be communicated to the employee at the earliest possible stage and the employee must have a right to reply prior to suspension. The employee may request the court to lift the suspension, usually in preliminary proceedings, and may also claim damages.

6.2 TERMINATION: INTRODUCTION

Termination of an employment agreement must comply with certain statutory rules, which provide for comprehensive job protection.[2] A distinction must be made between an employment agreement for a fixed period, and an employment agreement for an indefinite period. An employment agreement for a fixed period terminates automatically by law on the expiration of the agreed period (*see infra* Section 6.3). An agreement for an indefinite period is terminated by notice.

1. On the basis of BW Art. 7:611.
2. In 2005 the State Secretary for Finance implemented tax measures to ensure that the termination of the employment agreement of older employees would not boil down to an early retirement arrangement. If the latter was the case, employers had to pay high taxes over such arrangement (DG 2005/3299 and DGB2005/6722).

Such notice requires authorisation from the CWI, a governmental body (*see infra* Section 6.4).

Furthermore, an employment agreement for a fixed period and an employment agreement for an indefinite period can be terminated by mutual consent (*see infra* Section 6.5), during the trial period (*see infra* Section 6.6), for 'urgent cause' (*see infra* Section 6.7) or by court termination in case of 'serious cause' (*see infra* Section 6.8).

6.3 AGREEMENTS FOR A FIXED PERIOD

An agreement for a fixed period terminates automatically on expiry of that period.[3] Prior notice has to be given if this is a requirement of the employment contract. If employment continues after expiry of the fixed period, the agreement will be extended by operation of law under the same terms and conditions, and for the same period of time, as was stated in the original agreement, with a maximum of one year per extension.[4] Once an employment agreement for a fixed period has been extended, the employment agreement will terminate by operation of law when certain conditions are met. These are:

(a) the number of employment agreements must not be more than three (*i.e.* an employment agreement for a definite term, with two extensions for definite terms, succeeding each other within periods of not more than three months); or
(b) the total duration of the 'chain' of the employment agreements for a fixed period (which have succeeded each other within periods of not more than three months) amounts to not more than three years.[5]

If the number of employment agreements for a fixed period is more than three, or if the duration of the 'chain' is more than three years, the last employment agreement between the parties is considered to be an employment agreement for an indefinite period.

The 'theory of a chain of fixed period employment agreements' also applies to a situation where an employee continues his employment agreement with another employer, which – depending on the nature of the work – can be considered to be the successor of the original employer.

6.4 NOTICE OF TERMINATION OF AN AGREEMENT FOR AN INDEFINITE PERIOD

Notice by the employer of termination of an agreement requires a permit from the CWI[6] (*see supra* Section 6.2). Until this CWI permit is obtained, any notice is null

3. BW Art. 7:667.
4. BW Art. 7:668.
5. BW Art. 7:668 a.
6. Buitengewoon Besluit Arbeidsverhoudingen 1945 [BBA] (Decree on labour relations), Art. 6.

and void, and does not terminate the employment. An exception to this rule is notice of termination of the contract of a member of the managing board (*see supra* Section 5.3).

When applying for a CWI-permit the employer must specify reasons for dismissal. These reasons must be substantiated – the employer must provide evidence. The CWI then assesses whether the proposed termination is reasonable, taking into account the possibilities and interests of the employer and the employee, as well as other interests – more specifically related to the Dutch labour market.

Grounds for dismissal can be divided into three categories: economic grounds; grounds related to the employee's performance; and insurmountable problems in the relationship between the employer and the employee (sometimes related to the performance of the employee, sometimes not). In all situations it is up to the employer to convince the CWI that termination of employment is warranted. It is thus of the utmost importance to ensure that the application is properly drafted, well reasoned and thoroughly documented.

It is not uncommon for a permit to be refused. The decision of the CWI is irrevocable however, and not subject to appeal. The procedure is also time-consuming – normally taking from 5 to 10 weeks, or longer.

Should the employee become ill (or pregnant), the procedure is normally suspended until recovery (since it is prohibited to give notice of termination to sick or pregnant employees[7]). If the employer has obtained a permit and given notice of termination, the employee may still take the employer to court and sue for an adequate severance package (*see infra* Section 6.9).

Once the CWI permit has been issued, notice of termination may be given. The notice period prescribed by law, in a CLA, or in the employment agreement must be observed. Failure to comply with the proper notice period renders the termination 'irregular', although effective. Irregular termination entitles the employee to statutory damages.[8] These damages equal the employee's salary for the number of days for which notice would have been required. An important side effect of irregular termination is that the employee will not be bound to any non-competition clause in the employment agreement.[9]

It is not possible to give notice of termination to employees who fulfil certain requirements or for whom certain conditions apply;[10] *e.g.* an employee who is pregnant, ill (in the first two years of illness), [in military service,] or a member of a works council. If notice is given under such circumstances, the dismissed employee may nullify the notice by writing a letter to that effect.

The parties may agree to a notice period, provided that the statutory minimum period of notice is complied with. If no notice period had been agreed on and notice

7. BW Art. 7:670.
8. BW Art. 7:677.
9. BW Art. 7:653.
10. BW Art. 7:670.

is served by the employer, the statutory notice period is dependant on the number of years of service, as follows:[11]

(a) for a period of less than 5 years: 1 month;
(b) 5 to 10 years: 2 months;
(c) 10 to 15 years: 3 months;
(d) 15 years or more: 4 months.

The statutory notice periods may be extended by agreement. The notice to be given by the employee may not exceed six months, and the employer's period of notice is double that of the employee. The above rules pertaining to notice periods can be set aside by a CLA.

The employee has a right to seek judicial recourse on grounds that the dismissal was 'obviously unreasonable' (*see infra* Section 6.9).

6.5 TERMINATION BY MUTUAL CONSENT

An employment agreement may be terminated by mutual consent. This should be confirmed in a written document signed by both parties. Dutch case law states that the employer should not rely too readily upon the acceptance of the employee to terminate the employment agreement simply by mutual (oral) consent. He should check whether the employee has understood the consequences of termination and is really willing to terminate the employment agreement. An employee will usually only agree a mutual consent termination in exchange for a severance package.

6.6 TERMINATION DURING THE TRIAL PERIOD

During the trial period (*see supra* Section 4.1), either party may terminate the employment agreement without prior notice and without a permit from the CWI (*see supra* Section 6.4).[12] Termination may take place with immediate effect, during illness or military service (*see supra* Section 6.4).[13] A termination during the trial period shall not give rise to a claim for obviously unreasonable dismissal (*see infra* Section 6.9). Case law shows, however, that employers should not use unethical reasons, *e.g.* reasons which will result in unequal treatment as courts tend to punish such abuse of the right to terminate during the trial period.

If an employee has been hired through an outside employment agency and is subsequently offered employment directly by the employer for the same job, a trial period is no longer allowed.

11. BW Art. 7:672.
12. BW Art. 7:652.
13. BW Art. 7:670b.

6.7 TERMINATION FOR URGENT CAUSE

An employment agreement may be terminated without notice and with immediate effect if an urgent cause occurs.[14] No CWI permit is required. For the employer, 'urgent cause' means conduct or characteristics of the employee which the employer cannot reasonably be required to allow. The law gives a number of examples of 'urgent cause':[15]

(a) misleading or false statements made in the job application;
(b) serious lack of competence in the performance of duties;
(c) theft, fraud, or crimes involving a breach of trust;
(d) false statements which damage the employer's reputation;
(e) intimidation;
(f) deliberate damage to property;
(g) divulging trade or professional secrets;
(h) gross negligence in the performance of duties.

The cause must be serious and sufficiently urgent to warrant immediate and irrevocable termination. It must be communicated as soon as possible to the employee, preferably in writing. A delay before termination will be regarded as evidence that the cause was not urgent (although a brief delay of some days for the purpose of consulting a lawyer has been accepted by the courts).

If the employee disputes the urgent cause termination in court, the employer must prove his allegations. The court may decide that the cause was not urgent enough to justify immediate termination and declare the termination void. Since no CWI permit was obtained, the employee would in principle be entitled to receive his salary from the date of the nullified termination until such time as the employment agreement would be properly terminated.

6.8 COURT TERMINATION FOR SERIOUS CAUSE

Either party may request a competent court to terminate the employment agreement on the basis of serious cause[16] (*see supra* Section 6.2). A serious cause may be an urgent cause that has not previously been invoked to terminate the employment agreement, or a change in the circumstances of such a serious nature that the employment should reasonably be terminated instantly, or at very short notice. The procedure is widely used as a valid alternative to the CWI procedure mentioned above.

All facts relevant to the requested termination must be presented to the court. Each party has the right to be heard. If the court grants the termination, it sets an

---

14. BW Art. 7:677.
15. BW Art. 7:678.
16. BW Art. 7:685.

effective termination date. This termination does not have retroactive effect. Neither a CWI permit nor a period of notice is required.

If the Court grants termination because of a change in circumstances, it may award the employee compensation if it deems this fair due to those particular circumstances (*see infra* Section 6.9). The procedure usually takes two to three months. The decision of the court is not subject to appeal.

It is generally felt that in cases where the performance of the employee is at stake, or where problems in the relationship between the employer and the employee have occurred, it is easier to get court termination than a CWI permit, especially if the employer has not prepared himself well in advance by 'building up the file'.

Since 1 January 1997 the Cantonal Courts have used a formula in cases of court termination for serious cause (*see infra* Section 6.8). This formula has become known as the Cantonal Court Formula (*kantonrechtersformule*) and is applied in court proceedings on the basis of Article 7:685 of the Dutch Civil Code (BW). An employee is entitled to half a month's salary for each year of service under the age of 35; one month's salary for each year of service between the ages of 35 and 45; one and a half month's salary for each year of service between the ages of 45 and 55; and two month's salary for every year of service over the age of 55. 'Monthly salary' means one-twelfth of the yearly income (one month at base salary), holiday allowance of 8 per cent, fixed 13-month benefits, fixed bonuses, shift payments and any structural overtime payments. In exceptional cases other benefit components may be taken into account.

Severance payment is awarded in the case of a 'neutral' termination. 'Neutral' termination means a termination which can not be attributed to the employer or the employee (*e.g.* redundancy of the job itself). The courts often apply a correction to the calculation. Depending on the circumstances, court awards may therefore be (considerably) lower or (also considerably) higher than the 'neutral version' described in the Cantonal Court Formula above. As of 1st January 2009 the Cantonal Court Formula has been changed by the 'Circle of Cantonal Court Judges' (Kring van Kantonrechters). The change results in lower compensation for employees. Newly added is that years of service before the age of 35 entitle an employee to half a month's salary. This used to be one monthly salary.

6.9 OBVIOUSLY UNREASONABLE DISMISSAL: THE SEVERANCE PACKAGE

If, despite compliance with the legal requirements, the applicable CLA, and the employment agreement, the effects of termination on the dismissed employee are 'obviously unreasonable', the employee may then seek redress in court. Severance payment may be claimed, or reinstatement requested. If the latter is granted (which rarely happens) the court may be requested to establish a lump sum payment to 'buy off' the reinstatement of employment. The limitation period on these claims is six months from the effective date of termination.

The law provides a number of illustrations of what may be considered 'obviously unreasonable':[17]

(a) when no reason (or only a mere pretext) is given for the termination;
(b) when, with due regard to financial arrangements made for the employee and his prospects of finding new employment, the hardship endured by the employee is disproportionate to the interests of the employer; and
(c) when termination deviates from a seniority rule ('last in, first out') in the particular enterprise (unless there are overwhelming reasons for such deviation).

There are no uniform, statutory rules for severance payments. Severance packages can either be paid as a lump sum, or periodically to supplement a lower salary in a new job, or top up unemployment benefits. These supplementing arrangements are often used in collective redundancies (*see infra* Chapter 7). In individual cases it is more usual, especially with regard to higher level employees, to make a lump sum payment.

In 'unreasonable dismissal' proceedings the compensation awarded by a judge can be calculated on the basis of the Cantonal Court Formula, but this is up to the court: it can also use another way of deciding upon 'fair' compensation.

17. BW Art. 7:681.

Chapter 7
Collective Redundancies

The 1976 Act on the Notification of a Mass Lay-Off (WMC) (*Wet melding Collectief Ontslag*) sets out a number of procedural rules that must be followed in order to obtain the CWI permit necessary to give notice. The Act applies when an employer intends to terminate at least 20 employees employed in the sphere of activity of a specific CWI within a period of three months. The Netherlands are divided in six regions for the purposes of the Act.

The employer must notify both the CWI, and the trade unions, stating the projected dates of termination, providing information about the employees to be dismissed, and the date on which the works council was consulted (*see supra* Section 1.6). The CWI can not consider the request for a permit until one month from the date of notification, unless this statutory delay endangers the possibilities of re-employment for the employees to be dismissed, or the employment of the other employees in the enterprise concerned. If a statement from the trade unions (stating that they were consulted on this matter by the employer) is attached to the employer's notification to the CWI, the request for a permit will be considered immediately by the CWI before the one month waiting period has elapsed.

If an employer does not give statutory advance notification, but requests permission from the CWI to dismiss 20 or more employees within a three-month period, the statutory delay is increased to two months. The statutory delay is intended to facilitate consultations between the employer, the trade unions, the CWI and, in major cases, the Ministry of Economic Affairs or the Ministry of Social Affairs and Employment. Such consultations will look into the grounds for the mass redundancies, the reasoning behind the proposed down-sizing and the contents of a 'social plan' (being an agreement between the employer and the trade unions on the rules to be followed in finalising the employment agreements and assisting the redundant employees to find new jobs). The most important issue dealt with in the social plan is normally the formula to be used in calculating severance payments (*see supra* Section 6.9). In practice the formula is generally less generous than the formula used in individual situations. This is partly due to the collective nature of the issue.

Selecting employees who will be made redundant is a very important issue. There is a crucial principle that must be complied with, which is that of the 'balancing system'. According to this, the people with comparable jobs who are to be made redundant are equally divided among five age categories (15-24, 25-34, 35-44, 45-54 and 55 and older). From each of those age groups the employee who was last in is the first one proposed for dismissal.

As soon as the CWI permits have been issued, the employees may be given notice of termination in accordance with the notice period (*see supra* Section 6.4).

REGULATION ON SHORT-TIME WORKING

Until recently the regulation on short-time working has only been applied in exceptional circumstances, such as lightning damage or fire. Deregulation can also be applied if a healthy company is confronted with serious problems as a result of the credit crisis. To be eligible to apply the regulation a number of additional conditions must be met such as a drop in turnover of at least 30%, evidenced by an auditor's rapport. The application must be accompanied by an undertaking from the employer stating that he will train and second his employees.

Part II
Works Councils

Chapter 8
Dutch Works Councils

The participation of Dutch employees in the enterprise in which they work is prescribed in a number of legal regulations of which the Works Councils Act[1] is by far the most important. Pursuant to this Act the employee representative body known as the Works Council (*Ondernemingsraad*) must be given an opportunity to render advice on important management and business decisions. Certain of these decisions may require the prior consent of the Works Council.

Unlike the situation in several other countries, Netherlands' law does not entitle employees to representation on the management board of an enterprise, nor does it entitle the Works Council to determine the allocation of profits. In 'large' companies (*see infra* Section 11.6) the Works Council is entitled by law to recommend nominees for appointment to the supervisory board and has a reinforced right of recommendation with regard to no more than one third of the supervisory board members.[2]

1. Wet op de Ondernemingsraden [WOR] (Works Council Act) Art. 2. The WOR was introduced in 1971 and was amended in 1979, 1982, 1984, 1990, 1995, 1996, 1998, 1999, 2001, 2004 and 2006.
2. BW Art. 2:158(5)(6)/268(5)(6).

Chapter 9
Establishment

9.1 DEFINITIONS

An entrepreneur maintaining an enterprise in which at least 50 persons are usually employed must establish a Works Council in the interest of the sound functioning of the enterprise, and for purposes of consultation with and representation of the persons employed in that enterprise.[1]

The Works Councils Act defines an 'enterprise' as: every organisation operating as an independent organisation in the society where work is performed on the basis of an employment agreement or an appointment as civil servant (which for this purpose includes persons employed by any governmental instrumentality on a contractual basis).[2] The Works Councils Act defines 'entrepreneur' as any natural person or legal entity maintaining an enterprise.

The definition of enterprise is the key definition. The Works Council is established in an enterprise as prescribed by the Works Councils Act, and represents the employees of that enterprise. If a dispute arises as to which employees are represented by a Works Council, the scope of the relevant enterprise will be the deciding factor in dictating how the dispute is handled. Any enterprise involved must be a labour organisation operating independently in society. 'Independent' does not mean that the enterprise could not be part of a group. It means that the enterprise must fulfil a certain function of its own in society and present itself to third parties under a trade name. A factory that does not sell its products to the outside world would not meet the definition of enterprise as set forth in the Works Councils Act.

The key role played by the enterprise within the legal framework is also shown in its relationship with the 'entrepreneur' as defined in the Act: it is necessary to

---

1. WOR Art. 2.
2. WOR Art. 1(1)(c).

define the enterprise before identifying an entrepreneur maintaining a particular enterprise. The entrepreneur may be a Dutch company, but may also be a foreign corporation owning the enterprise in the Netherlands through its Dutch branch office.

Whenever a reference under the Works Councils Act is made to the 'entrepreneur', they will be referred to in this book as the 'company' or 'management'. The Works Councils Act does not specifically provide that the enterprise is confined to the territory of the Netherlands. Working on the principle of territory in which Netherlands' legislation is applicable, only enterprises located in the Netherlands are covered by the Act. Activities of a Dutch enterprise outside the Netherlands may be considered for inclusion if they are directly managed by the Dutch organisation (from within the Netherlands) and still remain activities of a Dutch labour organisation. More substantial extra-territorial activities will normally be tied to a separate foreign enterprise. Such activities would thus fall outside the scope of Dutch employee participation rights. It must be noted, however, that the Works Council of a Dutch enterprise has the right to offer advice on proposed decisions of the company relating to the establishment, take-over or relinquishment of control of a foreign enterprise; or to important modifications in the cooperation with – or participation in – such foreign enterprise, if it is seen that there will be significant consequences for the Dutch enterprise.

9.2 JOINT WORKS COUNCILS

If a company or a group of affiliated companies own two or more enterprises employing 50 (or more) employees, it must set up a Joint Works Council for the enterprises 'if this would advance the proper implementation of the Works Councils Act'. As a result, all enterprises covered by the Joint Works Council are considered one enterprise under the meaning of the Works Councils Act. Prior to making a decision to set up a Joint Works Council the company must inform the particular Works Councils which will be affected. In the event of an objection by a Works Council or Works Councils, the Cantonal Sector of the District Court shall decide the issue. Alternatively, the company owning an enterprise in which 50 persons (or more) are employed may set up a separate Works Council for a specific part of that enterprise, if it will advance the proper implementation of the Act. Subsequently the part of the enterprise for which a separate Works Council is set up shall be considered a separate enterprise under the meaning of the Act. The Act thus makes it possible to reduce or expand the number of Works Councils within a certain enterprise or enterprises.[3] The Works Councils Act does not provide for a definition of a 'group of affiliated companies'. A company belongs to a group if this company is subject to control. In principle, a shareholding of more than 50 per cent leads to control. A dispute is, however, settled on the basis of the underlying

3. WOR Arts 3, 4.

factual circumstances. Again, the principle of territory entails that the rules laid down in the Works Councils Act only apply to the Dutch part of the group of affiliated companies. In joint venture situations, the joint venture belongs to the group which has control. If none of the joint venture partners has control, the joint venture does not belong to the group of any of the partners.[4]

9.3 GROUP (DIVISIONAL) AND CENTRAL WORKS COUNCILS

A company which has established two or more Works Councils must establish a Central Works Council for the enterprises involved if this will advance the proper implementation of the Works Councils Act.[5] The company must provide the Works Councils with an opportunity to express their views. If a majority of the Works Councils is against the proposed establishment of a Central Works Council, the Cantonal Sector of the District Court shall decide the issue. If the majority of the existing Works Councils demand the establishment of a Central Works Council, the company must cooperate (as long as it is determined that this will advance the proper implementation of the Act).

The Works Councils Act also provides for the option of establishing a Group Works Council. The rules are the same as those regarding the establishment of the Central Works Council. The reference to 'Group' in the Works Councils Act is rather confusing, as it regards the establishment of a Works Council at divisional levels. The Central Works Council refers to a Works Council which has been established at the highest level in (the Dutch part of) a group of affiliated companies. If a group has no divisional structure, it is unlikely there will be a need for a Group (*i.e.* divisional) Works Council.

The Central or Group Works Council only deals with matters which are of common interest to all the enterprises, or the majority of those for which the Central or Group Works Council has been established. The powers of the individual Works Councils with regard to matters of common interest are transferred to the Central or Group Works Council. A Group Works Council is in turn subordinated to the Central Works Council and may not address matters dealt with by the Central Works Council. Clearly, it is not always easy to assess whether certain matters are of sufficient common interest. In practice, disputes sometimes arise between the company and the Works Councils at various levels, and between Works Councils at two (or more) different levels.[6]

---

4. Supreme Court 14 March 2008, JOR 2008/94.
5. WOR Art. 33(1).
6. In its Judgment of 16 Mar. 2000, 2000 JAR No. 80 (Philips Terneuzen) the Enterprise Chamber of the Amsterdam Court of Appeal takes a rather strict view on the common interest test, *i.e.* more than 50 per cent of the relevant enterprises 'represented' by the divisional Works Council had to be affected by the decision to allow a right of advice to the divisional Works Council.

Chapter 10
Procedure

10.1 ELECTION: COMMITTEES

The Works Council consists solely of elected employees. Each Works Council has a minimum of three members (if there are less than 50 persons employed by the company), up to a maximum of 25 members (if there are 6,000 persons or more employed by the company).[1] The management of the company and the Works Council meet regularly at a 'consultation meeting'.[2] The Works Council meets during working hours whenever this is possible. The elected members of the Works Council appoint a chairman from amongst their number.[3] The secretary of the Works Council is appointed in accordance with the Works Council bylaws.

Works Council members are entitled to a set number of hours per year away from their jobs for the purposes of meetings and study[4] and will receive their full salaries for these hours and/or days.[5] The management and the Works Council must agree in advance on the total number of hours and days reserved for this allowance. At least 60 hours per year must be reserved for meetings, and at least five days per year must be reserved for study. If no agreement can be reached, any member of the Works Council (or of one of its committees) may request the Cantonal Sector of the District Court to rule on the issue after previous mediation by the Industrial Committee (*see infra* Chapter 13).

The Works Council must establish bylaws regulating those matters assigned or entrusted to it pursuant to the Act.[6] The members of the Works Council are elected

1. WOR Art. 6(1).
2. WOR Art. 23.
3. WOR Art. 7.
4. WOR Art. 18(1),(2).
5. WOR Art. 17(3).
6. WOR Art. 8. According to WOR Art. 48, a company required to set up a Works Council must establish temporary bylaws. These are often based on the model bylaws, prepared by the Socio-Economic Council.

by employees of at least six months' standing.[7] Membership is open only to employees of at least one year's standing.[8] Members of the Works Council are elected by a sealed, written ballot drawn up from one or more lists of candidates. A list of candidates may be submitted by[9]:

(a) an association of employees, which is active in the relevant enterprise (or type of industry) and which has among its members persons who are qualified to vote;
(b) the lesser of 30 persons or one-third of the number of employees entitled to vote, none of whom are members of an association which has submitted a list of candidates as set forth under (a) above.

The Works Council may, in its bylaws, establish standing committees to address matters involving such groups of employees or subjects as it may designate. The Works Council may establish committees for separate locations of the enterprise, as well as committees to prepare any subjects to be handled by it.[10]

10.2 CONSULTATION PROCESS

Consultation between management and the employee representatives of the Works Council takes place at meetings. These meetings are conducted for the company by the director or a member of the management board. The Works Councils Act defines this officer as the person who, either alone or jointly with others in the enterprise, directly exercises the highest authority in the management of the labour force.[11] If an enterprise is managed by a management board, the board decides which of the members shall consult with the Works Council.[12] Normally, though not necessarily, the management board of the enterprise will be the management board of the company; if a company runs more than one enterprise, however, it may well be that the two boards need to be distinguished one from the other and so the management board of the enterprise will report to the board of the company.

The Works Council and management must hold a consultation meeting within two weeks of a request of either the company or the Works Council.[13] At the consultation meetings the following matters *must* be discussed:

a) matters for which either the management or the Works Council feel consultation is desirable;
b) matters for which consultation between the company and the Works Council is required under the Act (*see infra* Chapter 11).

---

7. WOR Art. 6(2).
8. WOR Arts 6(3).
9. WOR Art. 9(2).
10. WOR Art. 15.
11. WOR Art. 1(1)(e).
12. WOR Art. 23(4).
13. WOR Art. 23(1).

The Works Council may also submit proposals to the management regarding these matters outside the framework of a consultation meeting. Such proposals must be submitted to management in writing and must be accompanied by explanatory material. Management shall not decide on such proposals until there has been at least one discussion at a consultation meeting.[14]

Unless the consultation meeting reaches agreement on the appointment of a permanent chairman, the representative of the company and the chairman of the Works Council will serve alternately as chairman of the consultation meeting.[15] The director or the member of the management board charged with the management of the labour force must attend each consultation meeting. If this member is prevented from attending the meeting, one of the other members of the management board may replace him.

If there is only one director, and he is prevented from attending the consultation meeting, he may be replaced by:

(a) a supervisory board member, if any; or
(b) a member of the management board of the parent corporation, if any; or one or more representatives designated by the members of the management board; or
(c) an employee of the enterprise who has the authority to conduct the consultation meeting on behalf of the company.

The director or the person replacing him is entitled to request the assistance of other members of the management board, the supervisory board, or the management board of the parent corporation, and employees of the enterprise.

A consultation meeting may be held only if the provisions of the Works Council bylaws pertaining to the holding of a meeting of that Council are complied with. All members of the Works Council may address the meeting.[16]

The agenda of the consultation meeting must set forth the subjects submitted to the secretary by management and the Works Council for consultation.[17] The secretary of the Works Council will be the secretary of the consultation meeting, unless otherwise decided by management and the Works Council. Management and the Works Council may make joint arrangements for the conduct of business at the consultation meeting.[18]

If the company is either an N.V. or a B.V., the members of the supervisory board of the company (if such board exists), or one or more representatives from among their number, must be present at the consultation meeting at which the general business of the enterprise is discussed. If at least half of the shares of the company is directly or indirectly held by another corporation for its own account, the members of that management board must be present at these

14. WOR Art. 23(3).
15. WOR Art. 23a(2).
16. WOR Art. 23a(1).
17. WOR Art. 23a(4).
18. WOR Art. 24(1).

consultation meetings instead of the supervisory board members of the company. The management board of the parent corporation may designate representatives for this purpose.[19]

10.3 JOB SECURITY AND CONFIDENTIALITY

The members of the Works Council are entitled to job security. The employer must ensure that employees within the company who are or were candidates for membership of the Works Council, as well as those who hold or have held such office, are not adversely affected (*e.g.* discriminated against, passed over for promotion or dismissed because of holding such office, etc.). Furthermore, the employer is not allowed to terminate the employment of an employee who is a member of a Works Council, who was a member of a Works Council during the preceding two years, or who is or was a candidate for membership of the Works Council, without the consent of the individual or the approval of the Cantonal Sector of the District Court, except in the case of a closure of the relevant business activities or termination of the employment agreement for 'urgent cause'.[20] The Court has to ensure that the reason for the proposed termination bears no relationship to the membership of the Works Council.[21]

The elected members of the Works Council, as well as members of the committees of that council and any experts present by invitation at meetings of the Council, are under an obligation to keep confidential all matters involving business affairs. Confidentiality must also be maintained if invoked by management or by the Works Council itself or if the need for confidentiality should be implicitly understood.[22] The secretary of the Works Council or of a committee of that council is under the same obligation to maintain confidentiality as a member of the Works Council.

10.4 EXPENSES OF THE WORKS COUNCIL

The expenses of the Works Council and its committees are borne by the company to the extent reasonably required.[23] The Works Council is entitled to invite one or more experts to attend a meeting for the purpose of advising the Works Council on a given subject.[24] The costs of hiring such experts, as well as the costs of litigation, shall be borne by the company only if management has been informed in advance.[25] Should management object to bearing these costs, the matter is referred

19. WOR Art. 24(2).
20. BW Arts 7:670(4), 7:670a, 7:678.
21. BW Art. 7:670(4).
22. WOR Art. 20(1).
23. WOR Art. 22(1).
24. WOR Art. 16.
25. WOR Art. 22(2).

to the Cantonal Sector of the District Court. The foregoing does not apply, however, if the company has agreed with the Works Council with respect to fixed costs that the Council and its committees will incur in a specific year. The Works Council may spend this fixed amount at its discretion. Costs exceeding this amount will be borne by the company only to the extent that it agrees to do so.[26]

26. WOR Art. 22(3).

Chapter 11
Information, Consultation and Consent

11.1 GENERAL

The Works Council and its committees are entitled to receive all information reasonably necessary for the performance of their duties. The information must be in writing if requested.[1] The company must in any case supply the Works Council with certain basic information (*see infra* Section 11.2) (financial and business information, information on social policy (*see infra* Section 11.3)) from time to time.

The Works Council has the right to be consulted in certain instances (*see infra* Section 11.4) but in other instances, may block proposed action by the company (*see infra* Section 11.5). Furthermore, when the company is a 'large' company, the Works Council has certain rights with respect to the appointment of members of the supervisory board (*see infra* Section 11.6).

11.2 BASIC INFORMATION

At the beginning of each term of office of the Works Council, management must provide the Works Council with information regarding the following matters involving the enterprise:[2]

(a) the corporate form of the company and its Articles of Association (only applicable if the enterprise is owned by a legal entity);
(b) if the enterprise is owned by a natural person or one of several types of partnership entities recognised under the laws of the Netherlands, the name and address of this person or these managing partners;

---

1. WOR Art. 31(1).
2. WOR Art. 31(2).

(c) if the enterprise is owned by a legal entity, the names and addresses of the members of the supervisory and management boards;
(d) if the company is one of a number of companies affiliated in a group, the identities of the companies comprising that group, the allocation of control among them, and the names and addresses of those who (as a result of such allocation) may exercise control over the company;
(e) any other company or institution with which the company (other than by reason of the allocation of control under (d) above) maintains long-term relations which may be of vital importance to the continued existence of the enterprise, as well as the names and addresses of those who, as a result of such relations, may exercise control over the company;
(f) the organisation of the enterprise, names and addresses of the members of the management board and others exercising major managerial functions, and the manner in which responsibilities are allocated amongst those persons.

Management must inform the Works Council as soon as possible of any changes in the foregoing information.[3]

11.3 FINANCIAL AND BUSINESS INFORMATION: INFORMATION ON CERTAIN CONTEMPLATED ACTIONS: INFORMATION ON SOCIAL POLICY: INFORMATION ON REMUNERATION LEVELS AND EMPLOYMENT CONDITIONS

At least twice a year the company must furnish the Works Council with general information about the operations and results of the enterprise over the period elapsed, with special reference to the matters set forth in Section 11.4.a. This is intended to facilitate discussion about the general direction of the business.[4] At these bi-annual meetings, management must inform the Works Council about the operations and results of the company over the period elapsed, and about any anticipated action to deal with matters requiring prior consultation with, or consent of, the Works Council. The parties shall try to agree at what moment and in which manner the Works Council shall be engaged in the decision-making process with respect to these issues.[5]

If the company is an N.V. or a B.V., a cooperative society, or a mutual insurance fund, it must submit the annual accounts together with the annual report and any other data required by the Civil Code to the Works Council for discussion as soon as possible after adoption.[6]

3. WOR Art. 31(3).
4. WOR Art. 31a(1).
5. WOR Art. 24(1).
6. WOR Art. 31a(2).

If the N.V. or B.V. is a 'large' company (*see infra* Section 11.6) the annual accounts, annual report and other financial data must be given to the Works Council concurrently with their submission to the shareholders' meeting.

If the financial information pertaining to a company which is part of a group of affiliated companies is included in consolidated accounts of the group, the foregoing applies to the consolidated accounts of the group, the group's annual report, and any other data referred to in the Civil Code. In this case the Works Council must be supplied with sufficient additional written information to enable it to determine the extent to which the enterprise for which it was established has contributed to the aggregate result. If the company is part of a group of affiliated companies, and its financial information is not included in the consolidated accounts of the group, the Works Council must be given such written information as will enable it to determine the aggregate results of the group.[7] If a company's annual accounts relate to more than one enterprise, the Works Council must also be given sufficient written information to enable it to determine the extent to which the enterprise for which it was established has contributed to the aggregate result.[8]

If the company is not an N.V., a B.V., a cooperative society, or a mutual insurance fund (and therefore not required by the Civil Code to prepare annual accounts), the Works Council must be given alternative written information as specified by government regulation.[9] The company must provide the Works Council with information regarding its expectations for the financial and commercial future of the enterprise over the next six months at least twice a year, with special reference to the types of matters referred to below which (may) require consultation with the Works Council, as well as all domestic and foreign capital investments.[10] The company must also provide the Works Council with information about long-term plans, if any, and their anticipated consequences.[11]

Each year the company must provide the Works Council with written general information, including facts and figures, regarding the employment situation in the enterprise, as well as the social policy conducted by it during the preceding year. At the same time it must provide oral or written information on any projected changes in staff numbers and a summary of the social policy for the coming year.[12] The foregoing information must be discussed at a consultation meeting.

At least once per year a company with 100 employees or more must provide the Works Council with written information about remuneration levels and the contents of employment conditions per identifiable group of employees. The breakdown of groups must be dealt with at company level. For privacy reasons, a group of employees should at least consist of five persons. The information must

7. WOR Art. 31a(3).
8. WOR Art. 31a(4).
9. The Regulation on Financial Information for Works Councils provides that, within six months after the end of the financial year, the Works Council must be supplied with annual accounts and explanatory notes thereto, prepared in accordance with the provisions of the regulation.
10. WOR Art. 31a(6).
11. WOR Art. 31a(7).
12. WOR Art. 31b.

make clear to what extent the remuneration levels and employment conditions deviate from the previous year. The relevant obligation also applies to the remuneration levels and employment conditions of the management board and supervisory board of the company.[13] Companies meeting certain criteria for small or mid-sized companies are exempted.[14]

11.4 MATTERS REQUIRING PRIOR CONSULTATION

a Statutory Requirements

The company must give the Works Council an opportunity to offer advice on any decision it proposes to make involving:[15]

(a) transfer of control of the enterprise or any part thereof;
(b) the establishment, take-over or relinquishment of control of another enterprise; or the setting-up, substantial modification, or discontinuation of long-term cooperation with other enterprises, including the setting-up, modification or discontinuation of substantial financial participation by or on behalf of such an enterprise;
(c) discontinuation of the activities, or of a major part of the activities, of the enterprise;
(d) a substantial change in the activities of the enterprise;
(e) a substantial change in the organisation of the enterprise, or in the allocation of responsibility within the enterprise;
(f) change of the location of the enterprise;
(g) the recruitment or hiring of groups of workers;
(h) any major capital investment on behalf of the enterprise;
(i) seeking of substantial credit on behalf of the enterprise;
(j) the granting of substantial credit, and provision of security for substantial debts of another company, unless within the ordinary course of business of the enterprise;
(k) the introduction or modification of a major technological facility;
(l) any action or decisions on major measures of the enterprise regarding care for the environment, including introduction of new or modification of any existing policy, and any organisational or administrative facility relating to the environment;
(m) the adoption of an arrangement pertaining about bearing particular risks related to allowances paid to disabled employees as referred to in Article 40 of the Financing of Social Security Act;

13. WOR Art. 31d.
14. *See* BW Arts 2:396 and 2:397.
15. WOR Art. 25(1).

(n) the appointment and formulation of terms of reference for an outside expert to provide advice on any of the foregoing.

The substantiality test depends *inter alia* on the size and nature of the enterprise, and focuses on decisions which are of a more unusual nature than the day-to-day management of the company. A change in the activities of the enterprise which does not directly involve important consequences may nevertheless be considered substantial because of its long-term structural effects.

Paragraphs (b) and (n) above, insofar as the advice of the outside expert under (n) relates to any matter referred to under (b) do not apply if another enterprise is (or will be) established abroad, and if it cannot be reasonably expected that the proposed decision will lead to changes under paragraphs (c) through (f) above with regard to an enterprise maintained in the Netherlands.[16]

The advice of the Works Council must be requested by management early enough to allow it to have a significant influence on the proposed decision.[17] The request for advice must be accompanied by a detailed summary of the reasons for the relevant proposed decision, the anticipated effects on the employees and any proposed measures to be taken in response thereto.[18] In practice, it is not always easy to know when to seek advice. Clearly, there can be tension between providing an opportunity to influence the decision-making process, and the necessity to provide all the reasons and consequences of a specific proposed decision.

The Works Council may not give its advice until there has been at least one consultation meeting on the matter.[19] After the Works Council has submitted its advice, management may make a decision, and the Works Council shall be notified in writing as soon as possible. If the advice has not been followed or has been only partially followed, the Works Council will, at the same time, be informed why its advice was not followed.[20]

b Appeal

If the company has made a decision involving one of the matters referred to in Section 11.4.a that is contrary to advice given by the Works Council, or if facts and circumstances become known which, had they been known to the Works Council at the time of presenting its advice, might have led to a different result, the Works Council may appeal to the Enterprise Chamber of the Amsterdam Court of Appeal[21] within one month of management's written notification of the decision.

16. WOR Art. 25(1).
17. WOR Art. 25(2).
18. WOR Art. 25(3).
19. WOR Art. 25(4).
20. WOR Art. 25(5).
21. WOR Art. 26. The Enterprise Chamber is established at the Amsterdam Court by the Minister of Justice. The Enterprise Chamber consists of legally-trained members of the Court and two expert lay members who are not members of the Court.

During this one month period the company must suspend the implementation of the decision.[22]

The only available ground for appeal is that the company could not have reasonably reached the decision had it properly weighed up the interests involved.[23] Because of this limited scope of review, appeals are not readily granted on substantive issues. Procedural inadequacies, however, will almost invariably lead to a judgement favourable to the Works Council. Procedural inadequacies include, *e.g.* insufficient presentation of information, inadequate reasoning of a proposed decision, no proper discussion of alternatives presented by the Works Council, and/or failing to address the reasons for not following the negative advice given by the Works Council. The Enterprise Chamber has held that a company's failure to solicit the advice of the Works Council establishes an irrefutable presumption that the company could not have reasonably have reached its decision if it had properly weighed up the interests involved. If the Enterprise Chamber does find that the company could not have come to the decision in this manner, the Chamber may *inter alia* issue an order requiring the company to withdraw the decision, in whole or in part, and to repeal specified consequences of that decision.[24]

A problem may arise with respect to the rights of third parties conducting business with the enterprise. This may occur when the company has implemented its decision pending appeal, or implemented its decision without giving the Works Council an opportunity to render advice. Third party rights are in general respected and will not be affected by an adverse decision of the Enterprise Chamber, with the proviso that this may be different if the third party knew that at the time of its agreement with the company, the company was faced with a one month's suspension of the implementation of its decision. In addition, it could be held that rights of third parties may be affected if the third party was playing an active role in influencing the company to handle the matter vis-à-vis the Works Council in an improper manner. Works Councils often attempt to prevent the acquisition of rights by third parties by starting a summary proceeding to obtain a preliminary ruling under which the company is forbidden to implement its decision until the Enterprise Chamber has rendered its final decision.

If the Works Council is given the opportunity to formally advise the company and fails to do so, it may have lost its right to give advice. There is, however, no indication in either legislation or case law of the exact length of time within which the Works Council must respond to a request for advice. The vague standard applied is that the Works Council must render advice within a reasonable time. The reasonableness of a certain time frame depends on such factors as the complexity of the matter, the urgency involved, and the promptness with which information is likely to be provided by management.

---

22. WOR Art. 25(6).
23. WOR Art. 26(4).
24. WOR Art. 26(5).

c Proposed Decisions Involving the Appointment or Removal of the Director or a Member of the Management Board of the Enterprise

The company must also seek the advice of the Works Council prior to making any decision involving the appointment or removal of a director or member of the management board of the enterprise.[25] The matter has to be discussed at least one consultation meeting. The company is under no obligation to follow the advice given, and there is no right of appeal.

11.5 MATTERS REQUIRING PRIOR CONSENT

There are a limited number of matters regarding conditions of employment which are considered to be so important that they cannot be undertaken by the company without the prior consent of the Works Council.[26]

These include the introduction, modification or withdrawal of:

(a) arrangements involving pension insurance, a profit-sharing plan or savings plan;
(b) rules pertaining to working hours or holiday policy;
(c) a remuneration or job classification system;
(d) rules pertaining to safety, health or welfare in connection with work or absence through illness;
(e) rules pertaining to hiring, dismissal or promotion policies;
(f) rules pertaining to employee training;
(g) rules pertaining to employee performance review;
(h) rules pertaining to industrial social work;
(i) rules pertaining to work consultation;
(j) rules pertaining to the handling of complaints;
(k) rules pertaining to the registration, use and protection of personal data of the enterprise's employees; and
(l) rules for facilities aimed at observation or control of attendance, behaviour or performance of the employees.

The company must submit any such proposals in writing to the Works Council, together with a summary of the reasons for the proposal and the anticipated consequences to the employees. The Works Council is not able to take a decision until there has been at least one consultation meeting on the subject. After such consultation meeting, the Works Council must inform the company as soon as possible, in writing, of its decision with its reasons. The decision may be announced in a consultation meeting if either management or the Works Council so desires. After the Works Council's decision, management shall inform the Works Council as

25. WOR Art. 30(1).
26. WOR Art. 27(1).

soon as possible, in writing, what decision has been taken and the date on which that decision will take effect.[27]

The Works Council need not be consulted, however, if (and to the extent that) a matter that would ordinarily require the consent of the Works Council has already been dealt with in a collective bargaining agreement. Terms of employment drawn up by a public legal entity are treated for this purpose as a collective bargaining agreement.[28]

The company must advise the Works Council as soon as possible of its intention to seek the advice of an outside expert on any of the matters mentioned above.[29] If the Works Council's consent to a proposed decision is not obtained, the company may request the Cantonal Sector of the District Court to approve the decision. The Cantonal Sector of the District Court may only grant approval however if the Works Council's refusal to grant approval is unreasonable, or if the company's proposed decision is based on important business-organisational, business-economic or business-social reasons.[30]

Any decision by the company with respect to any of the matters set forth above, made without approval of the Works Council or the Cantonal Sector of the District Court, shall be rendered null and void, *if* the Works Council so advises the company. The Works Council must do so in writing, within one month of either: the company having notified the Works Council of its decision; or, in the absence of any such notification, within one month of becoming aware that the decision is being implemented or applied by the company.[31] The Works Council may request that the Cantonal Sector of the District Court forbid the company from taking any actions which would involve implementing or applying a decision which the Works Council has nullified. If the company believes that nullification of the decision has been unjustifiably applied, it may, within one month, petition the Cantonal Sector of the District Court for a decision on the matter.[32]

11.6 SUPERVISORY BOARD APPOINTMENT

If the company is a 'large' company (*structuurvennootschap*), it must appoint a supervisory board. A company qualifies as 'large' if the following three cumulative tests are met, or if the company has voluntarily adopted this status:

(a) the company's issued capital plus reserves, including its retained earnings, equal EUR 16 million[33] or more;

27. WOR Art. 27(2).
28. WOR Art. 27(3).
29. WOR Art. 31c.
30. WOR Art. 27(4).
31. WOR Art. 27(5).
32. WOR Art. 27(6).
33. This figure applies in 2008 and is adapted from time to time.

(b) the company or a dependent company[34] has established a Works Council; and
(c) the company, together with its dependent companies, normally employs 100 or more employees in the Netherlands.

Members of the supervisory board of a 'large' company are appointed for a four-year term by the shareholders' meeting on the nomination and proposal of the supervisory board.[35] The Works Council and the shareholders' meeting are entitled to make recommendations for these appointments.[36]

With regard to no more than one third of the supervisory board members, the Works Council has a reinforced right of recommendation. That means that the supervisory board allows the candidate proposed by the Works Council on its list of candidates, unless the supervisory board objects because it believes that the candidate is not qualified for board membership or that, as a result of the candidate's appointment, the supervisory board will not be 'properly constituted'.[37] If the supervisory board and the Works Council subsequently do not reach agreement, the dispute shall be reviewed by the Enterprise Chamber at the request of the supervisory board.[38]

11.7 AGREEMENTS WITH THE WORKS COUNCIL

Management and the Works Council may conclude agreements, generally known as '*convenanten*' *(covenants)*, for a variety of purposes. However, such agreements may not limit or restrict the statutory powers of the Works Council pursuant to the Works Councils Act. Many such agreements have been concluded in the restructuring of enterprises or in the context of a merger, or joint venture. Other examples include agreements for the desired 'profile' of the Supervisory Board (in terms of skills and background etc.) in 'large' companies.

In the restructuring of enterprises one common type of agreement is geared to a situation in which an international group with its top-holding company in the Netherlands intends to hive down its Dutch activities to a Dutch sub-holding company. In Dutch and international corporate practice, it is often felt that Works Councils of a specific country should not be in a position to be involved in matters which do not specifically relate to that country. Thus, it is practice in the Netherlands to aim to resolve this issue by 'pushing down' the (Central) Works

34. A dependent company is statutorily defined as (i) a legal entity in which the company, or any of its dependent companies, solely or jointly and for their own account, contributes half or more of the issued capital, and (ii) a partnership with a business enterprise registered with a Commercial Register in which the company or a dependent company is a fully liable partner towards third parties. BW Art. 2:152/262.
35. BW Art. 2:158(4)/268(4).
36. BW Art. 2:158(5)/268(5).
37. BW Art. 2:158(6)/268(6).
38. BW Art. 2:158(7)/268(7).

Council to national level only. A proposed decision in this respect is subject to the prior right of advice of the Works Council as long as this Works Council has been instituted at the level of the top-holding company when the decision is proposed. With a view to solving matters amicably it is not unusual to see that this pushing down of the Central Works Council to the level of Dutch sub-holding company is accompanied by an agreement with this Central Works Council addressing certain concerns on the side of the Central Works Council.

Chapter 12

Employee Participation in Small Enterprises

12.1 ENTERPRISES WITH FEWER THAN 50, BUT AT LEAST 10 EMPLOYEES

A company maintaining an enterprise with 10 or more, but less than 50 employees, and for which no Works Council has been established, has a minimum requirement to set up bi-annual meetings with its employees. A meeting must also be held at the request of one-quarter of the employees. Such request must state the reason(s) for the meeting. At least once a year the company must provide the employees with general information, orally or in writing, regarding the activities and results of the enterprise during the previous year. The company must also provide projections for the coming year. If the company is required to publicly declare its annual accounts and make an annual report, the employees shall be provided with copies of these.

Management must give the employees an opportunity to offer advice on any proposed action that may lead to: (i) the loss of jobs, or (ii) an important change in the nature of work, working conditions, or the circumstances under which the work is performed for one-quarter or more of the employees.[1] If management takes action contrary to the advice of its employees, it is not required to suspend the implementation of the action and employees can not appeal against any such action by management.

The Works Councils Act provides for an optional adoption of a body for employee representation (personeelsvertegenwoordiging), consisting of a minimum of three persons. At the request of the majority of the employees, management must institute such body. The employee representation body must consent to any introduction, modification or repeal of rules pertaining to (a) working hours

1. WOR Art. 35b.

or holiday policy, and (b) safety, health or welfare regulations in connection with work or absence through illness. The WOR provides for a statutory basis for the granting of additional powers to the employee representation body.[2]

12.2 ENTERPRISES WITH FEWER THAN 10 EMPLOYEES

The management of an enterprise with fewer than 10 employees and for which no Works Council has been established may institute an employee representation body as discussed above under 1. Any employee representation body must consent to any introduction, modification or repeal of rules pertaining to working hours or holiday policy. The WOR provides a statutory basis for the granting of additional powers to the employee representation body.[3]

2. WOR Art. 35c.
3. WOR Art. 35d.

Chapter 13
Judicial Recourse

In addition to the specific appeal procedures described in Section 11.4.b, the Works Councils Act sets forth a more general procedure to ensure compliance with the Act. In most instances, the Cantonal Sector of the District Court has jurisdiction over a demand for compliance with the Act.[1]

The Act provides, *inter alia*, that every employee entitled to elect Works Council members, and every association of employees may demand that management or the Works Council observe: the provisions of the Act involving the establishment of a Works Council; the determination of provisional regulations for that Council; the nomination of candidates for the Works Council; and the election of one or more members of the Works Council.[2]

The above applies only to the extent that implementation of the provisions of the Act is the responsibility of the company or the Works Council. These actions are treated as labour disputes. A condition for bringing this type of action before the Cantonal Sector of the District Court is that the aggrieved employee, Works Council, or company, first request mediation in writing by the relevant industrial committee.[3] Industrial Committees are semi-official organisations established by the Socio-Economic Council for groups of enterprises, on the basis of branch of trade or industry. Each Industrial Committee consists of an even number of members, half of which are organisations representing employers, and half are organisations representing employees. The Industrial Committee shall attempt to facilitate an amicable agreement without the intervention of the court. In the event that no amicable settlement is reached within two months of mediation having been requested, the Industrial Committee shall provide both parties with a written report on its findings, containing recommendations for the settlement of the dispute.

1. WOR Art. 36(2).
2. WOR Art. 36(1).
3. WOR Art. 36(3).

With the consent of both parties, the Industrial Committee may then extend the period for producing its report for a maximum of two months. Subsequently, either party may appeal in writing to the Cantonal Sector of the District Court within 30 days of the Industrial Committee having provided both parties with its findings, but in any case no later than 30 days after the expiration of the (extended) period of two months (as referred to above). The report of the findings and the Industrial Committee's recommendations shall be submitted together with the appeal.[4] The Cantonal Sector of the District Court may in its decision order the Works Council or the company to carry out – or refrain from carrying out – certain actions.[5]

4. WOR Art. 36(4).
5. WOR Art. 36(6).

Chapter 14

European Works Councils in the Netherlands

14.1 IMPLEMENTATION OF COUNCIL DIRECTIVE 94/45 IN THE NETHERLANDS

On 22 September 1994, the Council of the European Union adopted Directive 94/45/EC on the establishment of a European Works Council (EWC) or a procedure in Community-scale undertakings and Community-scale groups of undertakings for the purposes of informing and consulting employees (the 'Directive').[1] The Directive was required to be implemented by each Member State before 22 September 1996.

A draft statute incorporating the Directive into Netherlands' law was proposed to Dutch Parliament on 14 March 1996.[2] The ensuing debate focused on the limitations to the right of the EWC to information and consultation. The statute was adopted and entered into force on 5 February 1997 and was amended in 1990, and again in 1999.

On 2 July 2008, the European Commission made a proposal for a revised directive on EWC (a draft of an EWC Recast Directive). On 29 August 2008, the European social partners confirmed their support for the proposal of the European Commission as the basis for the revision, with only a restricted number of issues on which either side particularly considered that changes to that proposal should be sought. If the EWC Recast Directive is adopted in 2009, it will cause an amendment to the existing European Works Councils Act (hereinafter the 'Act') in the Netherlands.[3]

---

1. O.J. Eur. Comm. (No. L 254) 64 (1994).
2. Official Parliamentary Reports, No. 24 641.
3. Wet op de Europese ondernemingsraden [WEOR] (European Works Councils Act).

14.2 GENERAL OUTLINE OF THE STATUTE

The Dutch Parliament chose in 1996 to bring the provisions necessary to comply with the Directive into force in a separate Act. The Dutch legislator separated the rules pertaining to the EWC from Dutch legislation on co-determination of rights pursuant to the existing Works Councils Act for two reasons. First, the Directive says that the rights of employees to information and consultation under national law should not be prejudiced.[4] A separate act would emphasise that the Dutch Works Councils under existing Dutch legislation cannot be considered subordinate to the EWC. The EWC is not considered the 'top' consultative body, and the Dutch Works Councils have considerably more authority on a national level. The second reason is that these two acts define what constitutes an 'undertaking' or 'group' differently. The definitions set forth in the Directive of 22 September 1994 are used in the Act.

The Act is divided into four chapters. Chapter 1 provides definitions, addresses the protection of members of the Special Negotiating Body ('SNB') and EWC working in the Netherlands, rules of confidentiality and deals with the issue of jurisdiction. Chapter 2 contains important provisions on setting up a SNB, its rights and obligations; the negotiations for an agreed EWC, or procedure for informing and consulting employees or their representatives and related minimum requirements; and the provisions regarding the subsidiary requirements concerning information and consultation in the absence of an agreement. This chapter applies to a Community-scale undertaking – or controlling undertaking – having its domicile or registered offices in the Netherlands. It also applies to a Community-scale undertaking or controlling undertaking which has its domicile or registered offices outside the Member States, in as far as the management of the Dutch group undertaking has been appointed as the central management for the purpose of this Act or, in the absence of such appointment, is considered the central management because the number of employees in the Dutch group undertaking is greater than the number in other Member States.

Chapter 3 regulates the appointment of the Dutch members to a SNB of a EWC established in one of the other Member States. Finally, Chapter 4 focuses on dealing with agreements referred to as 'Article 13 Directive Agreements' and the treatment of Member States in which the Directive has not been implemented in its legislation.

14.3 SUBSTANTIVE OR PROCEDURAL PROVISIONS AT VARIANCE WITH THE DIRECTIVE

The Dutch Government explicitly stated its objective wish to follow the Directive closely. This objective was repeated during the legislative proceedings. The debate

4. Directive 94/45/EC Art. 12(2).

in Parliament on 28 August 1996, concerning the limitations to the right of the EWC to information and consultation focused on that issue and resulted in an agreement between the Minister of Social Affairs and the Second Chamber of Parliament, to explicitly provide in the Act that the competence of the EWC would be limited to matters concerning the undertakings or group undertakings located in the Member States. The following differences between the Act and the Directive can be identified.[5]

a Number of Members of the SNB and EWC

According to Article 5.2.b of the Directive, the SNB shall have a maximum of 17 members. Article 9.1 of the Act differs from this and says that this number may be exceeded.

Article 1.c of the Annex to the Directive says that the maximum number of EWC members shall be 30. Having regard to the present number of Member States, the Act follows the Directive in this respect as it will not be possible to cross the threshold of 30 when calculating the number of EWC members in accordance with Article 16 of the Act.

b Subsidiary Requirements: The Issue of Environmental Care

Article 2, second paragraph, of the Annex to the Directive mentions specific issues to be addressed in the meeting between the central management or its appointees and the EWC. Article 19.2 of the Act adds the issue of environmental care to the list.

c Subsidiary Requirements: Obligation to Inform and Consult in Time

This differs from the Annex to the Directive in that the Act specifically provides that, in the event of exceptional circumstances affecting the interests of the employees, a meeting to address such circumstances shall take place at a time when information and consultation can still influence the decision-making process.[6]

5. Differences on dealing with Art. 13 Directive Agreements are discussed in Section 14.12.
6. WEOR Art. 19(2).

14.4 GOVERNING LAW ISSUES

The Act applies to Dutch Community-scale undertakings and groups.[7] Community-scale undertakings and groups are deemed 'Dutch' if:

(a) the Community-scale undertaking or the controlling undertaking has its domicile or registered office in the Netherlands; or
(b) when a Community-scale undertaking or a controlling undertaking has its domicile or registered office outside any of the Member States, the central management as defined in Article 1, second and third paragraph, of the Act, has its domicile or registered office in the Netherlands.[8]

The law which applies to an undertaking will determine whether that undertaking is a controlling undertaking.[9] If that law is not the law of a Member State, this is determined by the law which applies to the group undertaking of which the management represents the controlling undertaking by virtue of Article 1.3 of the Act.[10]

The Act does not provide a definition of an 'employee' itself, but refers the definition to the law of the Member State in which the respective employee works.[11] Insofar as persons working in the Community-scale undertaking or group in the Netherlands are concerned, employees are defined as persons working in such an undertaking or group in the Netherlands by virtue of an employment agreement. It is not required that this employment agreement be entered into with the relevant undertaking. Consequently, persons working in the Community-scale undertaking or group by virtue of an employment agreement with, *e.g.* a secondment agency, or on the basis of any other type of assignment by a third party, are also taken into account.

With respect to the definition of 'employees, representatives', the Act takes the same approach: the definition is referred to the law of the Member State in which the relevant employees work.[12] If those employees work in the Netherlands, their representatives are defined as Dutch Works Councils established by virtue of the Dutch Works Councils Act. Thus, in this respect, the role of the trade unions in the Netherlands is ruled out.

7. WEOR Art. 6.
8. The original draft of the Act provided that if the controlling undertaking had its domicile or registered office outside the Member States, the management of its European holding company would automatically become the central management for the purposes of the Act. As a consequence, only if there was no such European holding company did the controlling undertaking have the right to choose its own representative. This provision was withdrawn during legislative proceedings.
9. As referred to in WEOR Art. 2(1).
10. WEOR Art. 2(6). *See* WEOR Art. 2(7) if more than one undertaking of a group satisfies the criteria set by WEOR Art. 2(1).
11. WEOR Art. 3(1).
12. WEOR Art. 3(2).

Each member of the SNB shall be elected or appointed in accordance with the law of the Member State in which he is employed.[13] The members of a EWC established under the subsidiary requirements are, in the absence of an agreement, elected or appointed in accordance with the law of the Member State in which such members are employed.[14] This rule does not apply if an agreement on the establishment of a EWC has been reached between the central management and the SNB. The Act allows a tailor-made approach with regard to the election or appointment of members of the agreed EWC.

If an SNB or a EWC is established in a Member State other than the Netherlands, their 'Dutch' members are appointed or elected in accordance with the rules laid down in the Act.[15] The rules provided by the Act on protection, continued pay and confidentiality also apply to those members working in the Netherlands.[16]

14.5 THE COMMUNITY-SCALE UNDERTAKING OR GROUP

An undertaking is considered to have a Community-scale dimension if, for the two preceding years, it had 150 employees or more in each of two Member States and, in the aggregate, 1,000 employees or more within all the Member States.[17]

A group of undertakings is considered to be of Community-scale dimension if it is made up of one controlling undertaking and one or more group undertakings of which two or more are established in different Member States and, for the two preceding years, at least one undertaking had an average of at least 150 employees in one Member State and another an average of at least 150 employees in another Member State. All group undertakings together must have had, in the aggregate; for the two preceding years 1,000 or more employees within all the Member States.[18]

Unless agreed otherwise,[19] the EWC should be established at the highest possible group level, *i.e.* the level of the controlling undertaking as defined in Article 2 of the Act.[20] Article 2.1 of the Act defines the controlling undertaking as one which can exercise a dominant influence, directly or indirectly, over another

13. WEOR Art. 9(2).
14. WEOR Art. 16(3).
15. WEOR Art. 23, in conjunction with WEOR Arts 10, 17.
16. WEOR Art. 4.
17. WEOR Art. 1(1)(c).
18. WEOR Art. 1(1)(d).
19. WEOR allows agreements between the central management and the SNB with EWC's or procedures for separate parts of the Community-scale undertaking or group: WEOR Art. 11(5).
20. If the controlling undertaking has its domicile or registered offices outside the Member States, it may designate as its representative the management of a group undertaking having its residence or seat within the Member States. In the absence of such designated representation, the EWC must be established at the level of the group undertaking with the greatest number of employees in one Member State.

undertaking within a Community-scale group and which itself is not an undertaking subject to direct or indirect dominant influence by another undertaking. An undertaking shall be assumed to be a controlling undertaking unless the contrary becomes apparent, if it:

(a) can appoint more than half of the members of the administrative, managing or supervisory body of the other undertaking; or
(b) controls a majority of the voting rights in the general meeting of the other undertaking; or
(c) provides more than half of the subscribed capital of the other undertaking.[21]

If more than one group undertaking meets one or more of these criteria, the undertaking which satisfies the criteria under (a) is deemed to be the controlling undertaking, whereby the right to appoint the managing body takes preference. If no undertaking meets the criteria under (a), that under (b) takes preference over that under (c), without prejudice to proof that yet another undertaking has a dominant influence.[22] The factual circumstances thus prevail.

14.6 TIMEFRAME PROVIDED FOR WITH RESPECT TO THE ESTABLISHMENT OF AN SNB AND EWC

The central management[23] is obligated to establish a EWC if it demonstrates that it will not negotiate with an SNB within six months of receipt of a written request to establish an SNB by at least 100 employees (or their representatives) from a minimum of two undertakings or establishments in at least two different Member States.[24] Article 7 of the Directive refers to a 'refusal' of the central management to start negotiations. The wording used in the Act is more flexible. As the establishment of an SNB can be time consuming, it might be appropriate to grant a somewhat longer period for the establishment, unless it can be rightfully alleged ('demonstrated') that the central management has not, in good faith, taken appropriate steps to enter into negotiations. The Act primarily aims to stop delaying tactics.

In addition, the central management is obliged to establish a EWC (if it has not entered into an agreement with the SNB to establish either a EWC or a procedure for information and consultation) within three years of the receipt of the written

21. WEOR Arts 2(2)-2(5) provide for more precise rules regarding these criteria.
22. WEOR Art. 2(7).
23. For a Community-scale undertaking it refers to the management of this undertaking, while for a Community-scale group it refers to the management of the controlling undertaking. If this controlling undertaking has its residence or seat outside the Member States, the central management is the management charged with the actual management of the establishment with the greatest number of employees in one Member State, unless another central management has been appointed. WEOR Arts 1(1)(e), 1(2).
24. WEOR Art. 15(a) with reference to WEOR Art. 8(2).

request to establish an SNB and, in the absence of such request, the date of the establishment of the SNB by the central management.[25]

If a request to set up an SNB has been received, delaying tactics from central management can not extend the period during which a EWC must be established. The central management could be forced to set up a statutory EWC three years after the date of the request. This three-year rule applies, unless the SNB has decided either not to open negotiations or to break off negotiations already being conducted.[26]

14.7 APPOINTMENT/ELECTION OF MEMBERS OF THE SNB AND STATUTORY EWC

The Dutch members of the SNB shall be appointed, or their appointment shall be withdrawn, by the Dutch Works Council(s) set up at Dutch establishments or undertakings.[27] The Dutch members of the SNB do not necessarily have to be members of the Dutch Works Council(s) or employees. They may, for instance, be members of a union. It would, however, seem logical that the Dutch Works Councils choose to appoint one of their own members. The SNB must be made up of one member for each Member State in which employees of the Community-scale undertaking or group work, and one, two or three supplementary members for, respectively, each Member State in which at least a quarter, half or three-quarters of the employees are employed.[28]

The rules only apply with respect to Member States in which the legislation incorporating the Directive has entered into force.[29] The Act does not provide specific rules for the election of members of the agreed EWC. The Act therefore allows a tailor-made approach. This means that with the approval of both the central management and the SNB, the members of the agreed EWC would not necessarily have to be employees of the Community-scale undertaking or group.

The statutory EWC is made up only of employees.[30] If the Community-scale undertaking or group has less than 5,000 employees, the council must have one member for each Member State in which the Community-scale undertaking or group has employees, and one, two or three supplementary members for, respectively, each Member State in which at least a quarter, half or three-quarters of the employees are employed.[31] If there are 5,000 employees or more, the statutory EWC must have one member for each Member State in which the employees are employed and one, three, six or nine supplementary members for, respectively,

25. WEOR Art. 8(2).
26. WEOR Art. 15.
27. WEOR Art. 10(1).
28. WEOR Art. 9(1).
29. WEOR Art. 25(1).
30. WEOR Art. 17(2). Membership terminates by operation of law when the member ceases to be an employee.
31. WEOR Art. 16(1).

each Member State in which at least a tenth, a quarter, half or three-quarters, of the employees are employed.[32]

The Dutch members of the statutory EWC hold office for a period of four years.[33] They are elected by the Dutch Works Council(s). If no Dutch Works Council has been established, the Dutch member(s) of the statutory EWC shall be elected by the Dutch employees. The election shall be by secret ballot. Each employee has one vote. Unions acting as such within the undertaking or group involved, are authorised to submit a list of candidates, provided that they have consulted their members within the relevant undertaking or group about the composition of this list.[34]

14.8 JOB SECURITY AND CONFIDENTIALITY

The members of the SNB or the EWC working in the Netherlands are entitled to job security. The employer must ensure that the position of the employees within the undertaking who are or were candidates for membership of a SNB or EWC, as well as those who hold or held such office, are not adversely affected.[35] Furthermore, the employer is not allowed to terminate the employment of an employee who is a member of an SNB or a EWC, or who was a member during the preceding two years, or who is or was a candidate for membership of an SNB or a EWC, without the consent of the individual or the approval of the Cantonal Sector of the District Court, except in the case of closure of the relevant business activities or termination of the employment agreement for 'urgent cause'.[36] The Court has to ensure that the reason for the proposed termination bears no relationship to the membership of the SNB or the EWC.[37]

The members of the SNB and the EWC are under a strict obligation of confidentiality.[38] The central management is not required to provide information to the SNB, or to the agreed or statutory EWC or procedure, in so far as this could reasonably be expected to seriously prejudice or harm the functioning of the Community-scale undertaking or group.[39]

14.9 MINIMUM REQUIREMENTS FOR AGREED ARRANGEMENTS

Subject to certain minimum requirements, the Act offers central management and the SNB ample freedom to tailor any agreed arrangement, to either an agreed EWC

32. WEOR Art. 16(2).
33. WEOR Art. 17(1).
34. WEOR Art. 10(5).
35. WEOR Art. 4(7).
36. BW Arts 7:670(4), 7:670a, 7:678.
37. BW Art. 7:670(4).
38. WEOR Arts 4(4), 4(5), 4(6).
39. WEOR Arts 11(7), 19(5). The Dutch legislator thus 'used' the possibility afforded in Art. 8(2) of the Directive to hold back certain information of a too sensitive nature.

or an agreed procedure, to meet their respective needs. The agreement to establish an agreed EWC shall regulate at least the following matters:

(a) the establishments or undertakings of the Community-scale undertaking or group for which the EWC was established;
(b) the size and composition of the EWC and the term of office of its members;
(c) the scope of the duties of the EWC and its authority;
(d) the manner in which the EWC is informed and consulted;
(e) the frequency, duration and venue of the meetings of the EWC;
(f) the financial and material resources at the disposal of the EWC.[40]

The agreement to establish an agreed procedure shall contain provisions on at least the following matters:

(i) to which establishments or undertakings of the Community-scale undertaking or group the procedure applies;
(ii) how employees or their representatives are informed and consulted on trans-border matters which (may) have significant consequences for the employees;
(iii) the manner in which the employees or their representatives can meet concerning the matters referred to under (b);
(iv) the financial and material resources made available for the implementation of the procedure.[41]

The central management and the SNB may agree that for parts of the Community-scale undertaking or group, separate agreed EWC shall be established or separate agreed procedures shall apply. Alternatively, they may agree that for one or more parts of the Community-scale undertaking or group, one or more agreed EWC shall be established, and one or more agreed procedures shall apply to other parts.[42]

Any agreed arrangement must contain provisions regarding the term of the agreed arrangement, the manner of negotiating a new agreed arrangement and the manner in which the agreed arrangement is to be amended to reflect any changes in the structure or size of the Community-scale undertaking or group, or in the numbers of employees employed in the Member States.[43]

---

40. WEOR Art. 11(3).
41. WEOR Art. 11(4).
42. WEOR Art. 11(5).
43. WEOR Art. 11(6). If the agreed arrangement does not provide that employees or their representatives of undertakings or establishments which became part of the Community-scale undertaking or group after the agreement was entered into are involved in the renewal or adjustment of the agreed arrangement within a two-year period, or if they are not represented in the agreed European Works Council or involved in an agreed procedure, central management must, upon the request of 100 or more of such employees or their representatives, establish a new SNB.

14.10 POWERS OF THE STATUTORY EWC

The powers of the EWC are limited to information and consultation on issues which are of importance for the entire Community-scale undertaking or group or at least two establishments or undertakings of the group in different Member States. The competence is limited to those matters concerning all establishments or group undertakings located in the Member States or at least two of the establishments or group undertakings located in different Member States.[44]

The central management meets at least once each calendar year with the EWC. In this meeting, the EWC is informed and consulted on the development of the activities and the prospects of the Community-scale undertaking or group. This information and consultation takes place on the basis of a written report. The information and consultation pertain in particular to the structure of the Community-scale undertaking or group, the economic position, the probable development of the activities, production and sales, the investments, substantial changes in the organisation, the introduction of new working procedures or production methods, environmental care, mergers, relocation, staff reductions, closure of undertakings or important parts thereof, the current employment situation and developments therein, and collective redundancies.[45]

In addition, the central management must inform the statutory EWC of all circumstances and proposed actions which could significantly affect the interests of the employees of at least two establishments or undertakings of the Community-scale undertaking or group in different Member States, in particular pertaining to the relocation or closure of the undertakings or collective redundancies.[46]

Upon the request of the EWC, the central management (or a more appropriate level of management having its own decision-making power) is required to meet with the EWC to inform and consult in more detail on the basis of a written report drawn up by the central management. This meeting has to take place at such a time that the information and the consultation will have a significant impact. The EWC (or a select committee) may render advice on the report at the end of the meeting or within a reasonable period after the meeting.[47] As set out above, central management does not have to provide information, in so far as this could reasonably be expected either to seriously prejudice or harm the functioning of the Community-scale undertaking or group. Central management may also impose an obligation of confidentiality should there be reasonable grounds for same.[48] Unless otherwise agreed, the meetings shall be chaired in turn by the central management and the EWC.[49]

---

44. WEOR Art. 19(1). These provisions are in conformity with Art. 1(a) of the Annex to the Directive.
45. WEOR Art. 19(2). This list is in conformity with that provided in the Annex to the Directive, with the exception of the reverence to the issue of environmental care, which is not dealt with in the Annex.
46. WEOR Art. 19(3).
47. WEOR Art. 19(4).
48. WEOR Art. 19(5).
49. WEOR Art. 19(8).

14.11 COSTS AND JUDICIAL RECOURSE

The SNB may call upon the assistance of one or more experts. The costs reasonably required for the performance of its duties shall be borne by the Community-scale or controlling undertaking. This only applies to the costs of consultation of one or more experts, or the costs of litigation, if the Community-scale or controlling undertaking has been informed in advance about the costs to be incurred.[50]

Similar rules apply to the statutory EWC. The obligation of the EWC to bear the costs of experts is, however, limited to one expert per item on the agenda, unless agreed otherwise with the Community-scale or controlling undertaking. Again the obligation to bear the costs also extends to the costs of litigation, under the condition that the Community-scale undertaking or the controlling undertaking is informed in advance of the costs to be incurred.[51]

Each interested party may request the Enterprise Chamber of the Court of Appeal in Amsterdam to determine that the provisions of the Act must be enforced, with the exception of disputes related to the job security of the Dutch members of an SNB or EWC. Such disputes are to be brought before the Cantonal Sector of the District Court.[52]

The Enterprise Chamber of the Court of Appeal in Amsterdam also has jurisdiction over disputes regarding the enforcement of agreed arrangements (an agreed EWC or an agreed procedure). The same applies for the enforcement of Article 13 Directive Agreements.[53]

14.12 ARTICLE 13 DIRECTIVE AGREEMENTS

Article 13 of the Directive provides that the Directive shall not apply to Community-scale undertakings or groups in which there is already an agreement in force providing for trans-border information and the consultation of employees. There is, however, one condition: the relevant agreement must cover the entire workforce.

Article 24.1 of the Act allows more than one Article 13 Directive Agreement per Community-scale undertaking or group. It is reasonable to assume as a consequence that in the view of the Dutch legislator the total number of Article 13 Directive Agreements would not necessarily have to cover the entire workforce of the relevant Community-scale undertaking or group. The Act clearly takes a different but also more practical approach compared to the Directive. This approach was approved by the Brussels Committee of Experts, instituted by the European Council to coordinate and enhance the implementation process of the

50. WEOR Art. 12.
51. WEOR Art. 20.
52. WEOR Art. 5 and BW Arts 7:670(4), 7:67a.
53. WEOR Art. 24(1): 'With the exception of Article 5, this Act shall not apply . . .'.

Directive. It still remains to be seen whether this will be accepted by the courts in other Member States.

Article 24.1 of the Act explicitly provides that, to be exempted from the application of the Act, the Article 13 Directive Agreement must be entered into with a representative body which could reasonably be considered a representative of the employees from the Member States in question. Article 13 of the Directive does not explicitly mention this requirement.

Article 24 of the Act says that the Act is not applicable to Community-scale undertakings or groups which, when the Act enters into force,[54] are party to one or more Article 13 Directive Agreements. The Act does not provide that such Agreements should have been concluded by 22 September 1996. Article 13 of the Directive clearly refers to agreements in force on 22 September 1996 or on the date of the incorporation of the Directive into the law of the Member State in question should this be before 22 September 1996.

If the Article 13 Directive Agreements do not include, or within five years after entry into force of the Act come to include, provisions to the effect that employees or their representatives of undertakings or establishments which joined the Community-scale undertaking or group after the closure of the relevant agreement, shall be involved within this five year period in the renewal or adjustment thereof, or shall be represented in the agreed information and consultation procedure, the Act applies after this five year period.[55] This means that central management would be under an obligation to set up a statutory EWC in accordance with the subsidiary requirements of the Act. Article 13 of the Directive does not contain such a provision regarding future developments. The Act would appear to be more flexible than the Directive, which merely provides that the agreement must cover the entire workforce.

54. The statute entered into force on 5 Feb. 1997.
55. WEOR Art. 24(2).

Selected Websites

Federation of Netherlands Industry and Employers
www.vno-ncw.nl
General information; services

Federation of Small and Medium Enterprises
www.mkb.nl
General information; services

Immigration Service
www.immigratiedienst.nl; www.ind.nl
Visa; employment

Labour Foundation
www.stvda.nl
General information; publications

Netherlands Trade Union Federation
www.fnv.nl
General information; news; reports

Social Economic Council
www.ser.nl
Tasks; social and economic advices

Offices of Allen & Overy

BELGIUM

Antwerp
Allen & Overy LLP
Uitbreidingstraat 80
B-2600 Antwerp
Belgium
Tel. +32 (0)3 287 7222
Fax +32 (0)3 287 7244

Brussels
Allen & Overy LLP
Avenue de Tervueren 268 A
B-1150 Brussels
Belgium
Tel. +32 (0)2 780 2222
Fax +32 (0)2 780 2244

CHINA

Beijing
Allen & Overy LLP, Beijing office
Suite 522
China World Tower 2
No. 1 Jian Guo Men Wai Avenue
Beijing 100004
PRC
Tel. +86 (0)10 6505 8800
Fax +86 (0)10 6505 6677

Hong Kong
Allen & Overy LLP
9th Floor
Three Exchange Square
Central Hong Kong
SAR
Tel. +852 2974 7000
Fax +852 2974 6999

Shanghai
Allen & Overy LLP
Shanghai office
18F Bank of Shanghai Tower
168 Yin Cheng Middle Road
Pudong, Shanghai 200120
PRC
Tel. +86 21 3896 5000
Fax +86 21 3896 5050

GERMANY

Duesseldorf
Allen & Overy LLP
Breite Straβe 27
40213 Düsseldorf
Germany
Tel. +49 211 2806 7000
Fax +49 211 2806 7800

Frankfurt
Allen & Overy LLP
Taunustor 2
60311 Frankfurt am Main
Germany
Tel. +49 (0)69 2648 5000
Fax +49 (0)69 2648 5800

Hamburg
Allen & Overy LLP
Kehrwieder 12
20457 Hamburg
Germany
Tel. +49 (0)40 82 221 20
Fax +49 (0)40 82 221 2200

Mannheim
Allen & Overy LLP
Erzbergerstraße 5
68165 Mannheim
Germany
Tel. +49 (0)621 3285 631
Fax +49 (0)621 3285 6541

FRANCE
Paris
Allen & Overy LLP
Edouard VII
26, boulevard des Capucines
75009 Paris
France
Tel. +33 (0)1 40 06 54 00
Fax +33 (0)1 40 06 54 54

HUNGARY
Budapest
Morley Allen & Overy Iroda
Madách Trade Center
Madách Imre út 13-14
H-1075 Budapest
Hungary
Tel. +36 1 483 2200
Fax +36 1 268 1515

ITALY
Milan
Allen & Overy
Studio Legale Associato
Via Manzoni, 41
20121 Milan
Italy
Tel. +39 02 290 491
Fax +39 02 290 49333

Rome
Allen & Overy
Studio Legale Associato
Corso Vittorio Emanuele II, 284
00186 Rome
Italy
Tel. +39 06 684 271
Fax +39 06 684 27333

Turin
Pavesio e Associati
*An independent law firm
in association with Allen & Overy
Corso Vittorio Emanuele II, 68
10121 Turin
Italy
Tel. +39 011 511 21
Fax +39 011 511 2333

JAPAN
Tokyo
Allen & Overy Gaikokuho Kyodo
Jigyo Horitsu Jimusho
Izumi Garden Tower, 34th Floor
1-6-1 Roppongi, Minato-ku
Tokyo 106-6034
Japan
Tel. +81 (0)3 5114 1600
Fax +81 (0)3 5114 1690

LUXEMBOURG
Luxembourg
Allen & Overy Luxembourg

58, rue Charles Martel
L-2134 Luxembourg
PO Box 5017
L-1050 Luxembourg
Tel. +352 44 44 55 1
Fax +352 44 44 55 222

THE NETHERLANDS
Amsterdam
Allen & Overy LLP
Apollolaan 15
1077 AB Amsterdam
PO Box 75440
1070 AK Amsterdam
Tel. +31 (0)20 674 1000
Fax +31 (0)20 674 1111

POLAND
Warsaw
Allen & Overy, A. Pędzich sp. k.
Rondo ONZ 1
34 floor
00-124 Warsaw
Poland
Tel. +48 (0)22 820 6100
Fax +48 (0)22 820 6199

ROMANIA
Bucharest
Radu Tărăcilă Pădurari
Retevoescu SCA
in association with Allen & Overy LLP
60 Dacia Boulevard
020061 Bucharest 2
Romania
Tel. +40 31 405 7777
Fax +40 31 405 7778

RUSSIA
Moscow
Allen & Overy Legal Services
Dmitrovsky pereulok 9
107031 Moscow
Russian Federation
Tel. +7 495 725 7900
Fax +7 495 725 7949

SAUDI ARABIA
Saudi Arabia
Abdulaziz AlGasim Law Firm
in association with Allen & Overy LLP
PO Box 89402, Riyadh 11623,
Kingdom of Saudi Arabia
4th floor, Al-Mada Centre Bld. No. 823,
Olaya, King Fahad Road, Riyadh

SINGAPORE
Singapore
Clifford Centre
Allen & Overy Shook Lin & Bok
24 Raffles Place
#22-00 Clifford Centre
Singapore 048621
Tel. +65 6435 7400
Fax +65 6435 7474

SLOVAKIA
Bratislava
Allen & Overy Bratislava, s.r.o.
Carlton Savoy Building
Mostová 2, 5th Floor
811 02 Bratislava
Slovak Republic
Tel. +421 2 5920 2400
Fax +421 2 5920 2424

SPAIN
Madrid
Allen & Overy
Pedro de Valdivia 10
28006 Madrid
Spain
Tel. +34 91 782 98 00
Fax +34 91 782 98 99

THAILAND
Bangkok
Allen & Overy (Thailand) Co., Ltd.
22nd Floor, Sindhorn Tower 3
130-132 Wireless Road
Lumpini, Pathumwan
Bangkok 10330
Thailand

Tel. +66 (0)2 263 7600
Fax +66 (0)2 263 7699

CZECH REPUBLIC
Prague
Allen & Overy, Praha
Advokátní kancelář
V Celnici 4
5th Floor
110 00 Prague 1
Czech Republic
Tel. +420 222 107 111
Fax +420 222 107 107

UNITED KINGDOM
London
Bishops Square
Allen & Overy LLP
One Bishops Square
London
E1 6AD
United Kingdom
Tel. +44 (0)20 3088 0000
Fax +44 (0)20 3088 0088

Canary Wharf
Allen & Overy LLP
40 Bank Street
London
E14 5DU
United Kingdom
Tel. +44 (0)20 3088 0000
Fax +44 (0)20 3088 0088

UNITED ARAB EMIRATES
Abu Dhabi
Allen & Overy LLP
PO Box 7907
Abu Dhabi
United Arab Emirates
Tel. +971 (0)2 418 0400
Fax +971 (0)2 418 0499

Dubai
Allen & Overy LLP
Level 2
The Gate Village Building GV08
Dubai International Financial Centre
PO Box 506678
Dubai, United Arab Emirates
Tel. +971 (0)4 426 7100
Fax +971 (0)4 426 7199

UNITED STATES OF AMERICA
New York
Allen & Overy LLP
1221 Avenue of the Americas
New York, NY 10020
United States of America
Tel. +1 212 610 6300
Fax +1 212 610 6399

Dutch Business Law Series

1. Marieke van Hooijdonk and Peter Eijsvoogel, *Litigation in the Netherlands: Civil Procedure, Arbitration and Administrative Litigation*, 2009 (ISBN 978-90-411-2855-3)
2. Ferdinand B.J. Grapperhaus and Leonard G. Verburg, *Employment Law and Works Councils of the Netherlands*, 2009 (ISBN 978-90-411-2858-4)